Creative Minds: production, manufacturing and invention in ancient Ireland

Proceedings of a public seminar on archaeological discoveries on national road schemes, August 2009

Edited by Michael Stanley, Ed Danaher and James Eogan

Published by the National Roads Authority 2010
St Martin's House
Waterloo Road
Dublin 4

© National Roads Authority and the authors

All rights reserved. No part of this book may be reprinted or reproduced or utilised in any electronic, mechanical or other means, now known or hereafter invented, including photocopying and recording, or otherwise without either the prior written consent of the publishers or a licence permitting restricted copying in Ireland issued by the Irish Copyright Licensing Agency Ltd, The Writers' Centre, 19 Parnell Square, Dublin 1.

Cover illustrations

Main image:
Andrew Murphy, the National Museum Wales blacksmith, in the smithy at St Fagans Folk Park, Wales. (Tim Young)

Smaller pictures (from left to right):
Experimental hand-spinning with a heavy stone spindle-whorl recovered from Lisleagh I ringfort, Co. Cork. (Richard O'Brien)
Reconstruction of an early medieval hand-bell based on excavated evidence from a monastic site at Clonfad 3, Co. Westmeath, on the route of the N6 Kinnegad to Kilbeggan Dual Carriageway. (GeoArch Ltd)
Traditional mound kiln being used to produce charcoal near Pondicherry in south-east India. Similar charcoal production kilns would have been used in Ireland in the late medieval and post-medieval periods. (Chris Adam)

Cover design: Wordwell Ltd

ISBN 978-0-9564180-2-9
ISSN 1649-3540

British Library Cataloguing-in-Publication Data.
A catalogue record for this book is available from the British Library.

First published in 2010

Typeset in Ireland by Wordwell Ltd

Printed by Castuera, Pamplona

CREATIVE MINDS

Contents

Foreword	vi
Acknowledgements	ix
Note on radiocarbon dates	ix
1. From boy to man: 'rights' of passage and the lithic assemblage from a Neolithic mound in Tullahedy, Co. Tipperary *Farina Sternke* *Freelance Lithic Finds Specialist*	1
2. Spindle-whorls and hand-spinning in Ireland *Richard O'Brien* *NRA Archaeologist*	15
3. Clay and fire: the development and distribution of pottery traditions in prehistoric Ireland *Eoin Grogan and Helen Roche* *Independent Consultants*	27
4. Ancient woodland use in the midlands: understanding environmental and landscape change through archaeological and palaeoecological techniques *Ellen OCarroll* *Wood Identification Specialist*	47
5. Reinventing the wheel: new evidence from Edercloon, Co. Longford *Caitríona Moore and Chiara Chiriotti* *Excavation Director and Surveyor and Illustrator, CRDS Ltd*	57
6. Iron-smelting and smithing: new evidence emerging on Irish road schemes *Angela Wallace and Lorna Anguilano* *Archaeometallurgist, Connacht Archaeological Services, and Materials Scientist, Experimental Techniques Centre, Brunel University*	69
7. For whom the bell tolls: the monastic site at Clonfad 3, Co. Westmeath *Paul Stevens* *Senior Archaeologist, Valerie J Keeley Ltd*	85
8. Charcoal production in medieval Ireland *Niall Kenny* *Archaeological Researcher, Archaeological Consultancy Services Ltd*	99
Appendix 1—Radiocarbon dates from excavated archaeological sites described in these proceedings	117
References	129

Foreword

The National Roads Authority (NRA) is pleased once again to publish the proceedings of our annual seminar on archaeology and national road schemes. The seminar is an established feature of Heritage Week. The 2009 event was particularly well attended and presentations on the day covered a range of interesting discoveries made in the course of excavations on road schemes in many parts of the country. This monograph is a permanent record of the seminar proceedings and so will help to achieve a key objective of the NRA—to bring knowledge and awareness of what is being discovered through archaeological investigation and excavation, integral elements of the national road-building programme, to local communities and the general public. This knowledge is a valuable legacy of the roads programme; it helps to promote awareness of our past and of our sense of place and who we are.

The scale of archaeological activities engaged in by the NRA over the past 10 years has no precedent in the history of the State. The National Development Plan (NDP), 2000–2006, and underpinning funding from government for investment in national road infrastructure provided the impetus and opportunity for archaeological activities at a level that could scarcely have been dreamed of by those involved in the profession. The challenges presented to the NRA were many and varied. Our established expertise in the area of engineering left us relatively well placed to meet the planning, design and construction aspects of the ambitious roads programme mandated by government in the NDP. But we were much less well endowed with the knowledge and expertise required to handle the archaeological dimension of what the NRA was then embarking upon. Our initial, tentative steps to address archaeology encountered some difficulty, and the lack of specialist management expertise in the area led to disruption of road construction activities on some schemes while archaeological excavations were completed. It was obvious that a more structured and planned approach was called for—one that would integrate consideration of archaeology into all phases of road scheme planning, route selection and construction. In this way we sought to ensure that archaeology received the attention it rightly deserved while also bringing efficiencies to the roll-out of the national roads programme.

The cooperative efforts of the NRA and the Department of Arts, Heritage, Gaeltacht and the Islands led to the adoption of a Code of Practice on archaeology and the national roads programme in 2000. This key development set the direction for the NRA's subsequent activities in the area of archaeology. The early steps to give effect to the Code saw the NRA recruit a small number of archaeologists, as well as a larger number who were then employed by local authorities to address national road-related issues.

The NRA interview board was especially impressed by one candidate, Dáire O'Rourke. Her knowledge, her infectious enthusiasm for her career choice and her track record at Dublinia and in her role as City Archaeologist with Dublin Corporation convinced us that Dáire was best placed to be the first person to fill the position of Head of Archaeology with the NRA. She joined the NRA in early 2001 and immediately applied her energy and expertise to devising practices and procedures, as well as management techniques, that over the intervening years have well served the interests of both archaeology and the national roads programme.

Dáire's leadership qualities were soon apparent as she sought to mould the disparate group of local authority archaeologists and NRA personnel into a professional, closely knit team in pursuit of common standards and objectives. Many of these individuals subsequently joined the NRA and have maintained the team spirit that developed in those early years. Dáire was also responsible for establishing a research fellowship and a publications strategy, aimed, respectively, at maximising the knowledge to be derived from excavations on national road schemes and making results available to as wide an audience as possible.

Illness deprived the NRA of Dáire's commitment and expertise in recent years. Following a hard-fought battle, characterised by inner strength and the preservation of her endearing personality and attributes, Dáire passed away in late April. She is sadly missed by her colleagues.

Dáire made an indelible mark on the NRA's approach to archaeology. Her legacy continues to give benefits in many ways, not least of which is this publication of last year's seminar proceedings. Let us dedicate this volume to her memory.

Michael Egan
Head of Corporate Affairs
and Professional Services,
National Roads Authority

This monograph is dedicated to Dáire O'Rourke,
Head of Archaeology, 2001 to 2010,
National Roads Authority.

Dáire was an elemental force who contributed greatly
to the Authority and to her profession.

She will be sadly missed by all her friends and colleagues.

A true Creative Mind.

Acknowledgements

The NRA would like to express its appreciation to Lorna Anguilano, Chiara Chiriotti, Eoin Grogan, Niall Kenny, Caitríona Moore, Richard O'Brien, Ellen OCarroll, Helen Roche, Farina Sternke, Paul Stevens, John Tierney and Angela Wallace for their contributions to the seminar and proceedings. The 2009 seminar was organised by Lillian Butler, Senior Administrator, Michael Stanley, Archaeologist, and Frantisek Zak Matyasowszky, Assistant Archaeologist, NRA. Eoin Scully, NRA, also assisted in the organisation of the seminar, and Michael MacDonagh, Senior Archaeologist, and Mary Deevy, Senior Archaeologist, NRA, co-chaired the event.

Michael Stanley, Ed Danaher, Archaeologist, and James Eogan, Senior Archaeologist, NRA, prepared the proceedings for publication. The authors, Archaeological Consultancy Services Ltd, CRDS Ltd, Irish Archaeological Consultancy Ltd, Margaret Gowen & Co. Ltd, Mayo County Council, University College Cork and Valerie J Keeley Ltd all kindly supplied illustrations. The monograph was copy-edited by Emer Condit and was designed and typeset by Wordwell Ltd.

Material from Ordnance Survey Ireland is reproduced with the permission of the Government of Ireland and Ordnance Survey Ireland under permit number EN0045206.

Note on radiocarbon dates

All of the radiocarbon dates cited in the following papers are calibrated date ranges equivalent to the probable calendrical age of the sample and are expressed at the two-sigma (98% probability) level of confidence. Appendix 1 provides full details of all the available radiocarbon dates from the excavated archaeological sites described in these proceedings.

1. From boy to man: 'rights' of passage and the lithic assemblage from a Neolithic mound in Tullahedy, Co. Tipperary

Farina Sternke

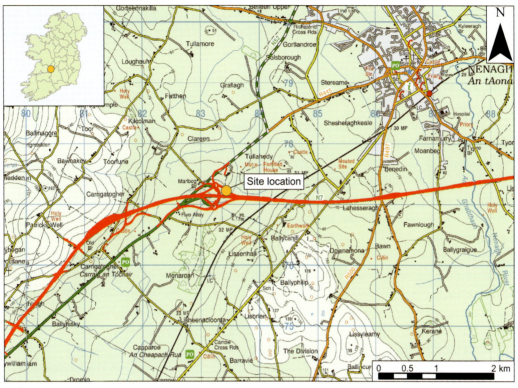

Illus. 1—Location of site at Tullahedy, Co. Tipperary (based on the Ordnance Survey Ireland map).

Specialist analysis of lithic (stone tool) assemblages from archaeological excavations is often viewed as a dry, technical pursuit. Behind the precise measurements and statistics, however, there can be a tangible connection with our ancestors (young and old) as their hands reach back to us from prehistory. This paper presents an important lithic assemblage excavated from a Neolithic (c. 4000–2400 BC) mound in Tullahedy, Co. Tipperary (Illus. 1). The excavations were carried out by the Department of Archaeology, University College Cork (UCC), under the direction of Hilary Kelleher in 2006 in advance of the construction of the N7 Nenagh–Limerick High Quality Dual Carriageway.[1] These works were undertaken on behalf of Limerick County Council, Tipperary North County Council and the NRA. The site had previously been partly excavated by Archaeological Development Services Ltd in 1997–8 in advance of the construction of the N7 Nenagh Bypass (McConway 1998; 2000).[2] Over 2,000 lithic finds were recovered during the initial excavation, including c. 150 polished stone axeheads and axehead fragments, which constitute approximately 55% of the entire collection of stone tools found at this site.

In this paper only the stone tools retrieved by UCC are discussed, but rather than presenting the entire assemblage (a detailed publication of the site is in preparation) the author will attempt to shed more light on the assemblage and the site in relation to the theme of transformation. It is clear that transformation was a major concern of the mound's inhabitants, both in terms of the location and the hitherto unknown technologies observed within the lithic assemblage. It is suggested that both relate to rituals associated with rites of passage in connection with the transition of an individual from childhood to adulthood. Focusing on the two most important manufacturing processes at the site, arrowhead and polished stone axehead production, it is suggested that parts of these processes relate to such rituals. Evidence of differential raw material use and production techniques and the presence of apprentices will be presented in support of this interpretation.

The excavation

The excavation of the assemblage discussed in this paper took place from March 2006 until January 2007 and uncovered the remains of an enclosed Neolithic settlement complex that was located on a peninsula jutting out into a former lake (Kelleher, in prep.) (Illus. 2). Unfortunately, the summit of the mound was quarried away in the 19th and early 20th centuries, and therefore what the top of the mound originally looked like and what activities took place there are unknown. Post-excavation analysis and interpretation are continuing at the time of writing, and so the outline of the development of the site presented hereafter is preliminary in nature. A definitive account of the Tullahedy excavations is currently being prepared for publication (Cleary, in prep.).

Thus far five main phases of site occupation or use have been identified. Archaeological features and deposits were uncovered on all sides of the mound; it appears that the entire site was used simultaneously and that it was divided into separate 'taskscapes' where different activities took place.

Phase 1, the main phase of settlement at Tullahedy, consisted of the creation of a hollowed-out basin in the south-eastern slope of the mound; this provided an artificial

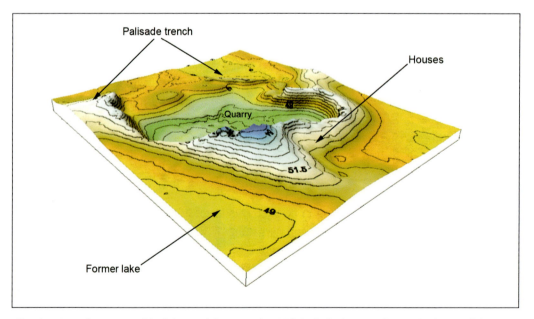

Illus. 2—Digital terrain model of the Neolithic mound at Tullahedy, looking north-west (Hilary Kelleher & Hugh Kavanagh).

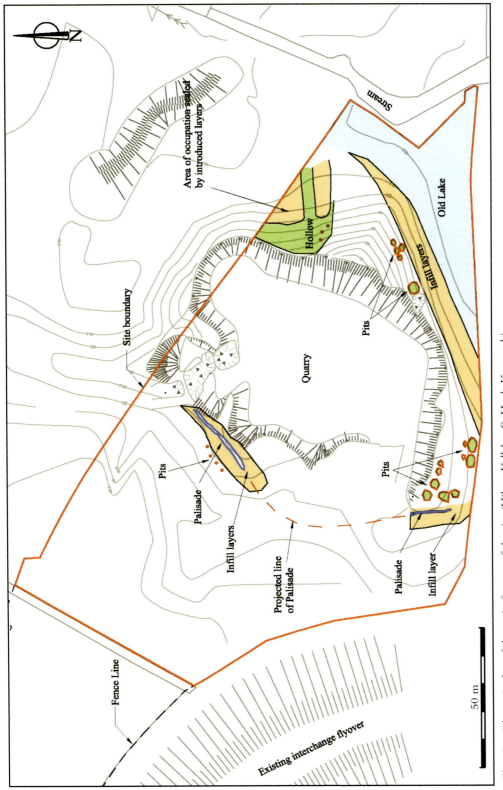

Illus. 3—Schematic plan of the main features of the site (Hilary Kelleher & Hugh Kavanagh).

shelter, within which two rectangular houses were erected. They were represented by a series of linear slot-trenches, with associated pits and hearths. The activities that took place here included food-processing, hide-processing and other related domestic tasks. Radiocarbon dating indicates that this settlement predominantly dates from the Middle Neolithic period (c. 3600–2900 BC; see Appendix 1 for details). A third house of similar outline was excavated on the southern slope, and a palisade on the north-western/western side of the mound is contemporary with the three houses.

During phase 2 one of the two houses on the south-eastern slope was covered with a charcoal-rich spread that contained organic remains such as hazelnut shells, cereal grains and seeds. Several other deposits overlay this spread. The natural mound was altered in the later Neolithic period (phase 3) through the introduction of several layers of locally occurring glacial till, possibly taken from the summit. These infill layers were up to 1 m thick and were used to fill naturally occurring hollows and alter the contours of the mound (Illus. 3) (Kelleher, in prep.). It thus represents the first known major Neolithic 'landscaping project' of this type in Ireland. Phase 4 constitutes the final period of prehistoric use of the site, during which two linear ditches were dug on the north-western side of the mound. Phase 5 is represented by modern activities related to the quarry and the construction of a stone and gravel trackway.

The site was extremely rich in artefacts, but the different types of stone tools and pottery recovered clearly reflect several periods of use throughout the Neolithic period. In addition, there is limited evidence in the form of diagnostic stone tools to indicate that the mound and its surrounding landscape attracted Early Mesolithic and Bronze Age settlers, which is to be expected given the nature and location of the site (see also McConway 1998; 2000). Access to a fresh water source such as a lake would have been a paramount concern for all prehistoric settlers and would have facilitated the establishment of short- or long-term settlements and the use of the surrounding landscape for domestic activities. The elevation of the mound would have provided commanding views over the surrounding landscape. In addition, later prehistoric settlers may have been aware of the significance of the mound and the wider ritual landscape. Thus it is not surprising that the stone tool assemblage from the site contains evidence for a continuity of place.

The stone tool assemblage

The stone tool assemblage from Tullahedy includes a flaked stone component and a coarse stone tool or macro-tool component. The latter refers to larger stone tools such as quern-stones, rubbing stones and polished stone axeheads. The flaked stone or lithic component typically includes smaller stone tools such as hide-scrapers, knives, simple flakes and blades and arrowheads that were produced during a process called 'knapping'. Knapping is the practice of splitting larger cobbles or nodules of stone into smaller pieces such as flakes and blades. These flakes and blades, generally referred to as blanks, may be used unmodified, for example as knives, or may be modified into specific tools, recognisable as distinct types such as hide-scrapers and arrowheads, through a process called 'retouching'. Retouching is best described as knapping on a very small scale. It involves the removal of very small flakes that are commonly referred to as small fraction waste or débitage. Knapping produces a wide array of by-products, some of which are diagnostic and can be linked to specific types of tool production when analysed, even if the finished tool is no longer present in an assemblage. For example, the small fraction waste produced during the manufacture of an arrowhead has particular characteristics and such manufacturing processes can be recognised at a site, even if the arrowhead was subsequently hafted and later lost during use elsewhere.

The stone tool assemblage discussed here comprises 1,691 pieces of stone, including 137 polished stone axeheads/fragments/flakes. The flaked assemblage consists of cores (stone lumps from which pieces are removed for tool production), modified and unmodified flakes and blades, large amounts of débitage and over 300 formal tools (Table 1) (see Sternke, in prep. a, for a full report and discussion of this assemblage). Larger stone tools such as quern-stones, hone stones, rubbing stones and hammerstones were also recovered. It should be noted that Neolithic assemblages of this size are very rare in the archaeological record of the southern half of Ireland, and this emphasises the archaeological significance of the mound at Tullahedy.

Table 1—Composition of the stone tool assemblage from Tullahedy.

Type	Number
Core	84
Blade	72
Flake	363
Waste (<2 cm)	558
Retouched artefact	336
Chunk	18
Quartz crystal	13
Bead	1
Macro-tools	67
Natural chunks	42
Total	**1,554**

Chert, which was most likely procured locally from secondary sources such as river beds (Beese, in prep.), accounts for 87% of the stone tool assemblage. (Chert is a black, grey or blue siliceous rock that occurs in the form of bands in limestone deposits and was often used for tool production in the midlands.) Large quantities of unmodified, fist-sized and smaller chert nodules were collected during the excavation, but their origin has yet to be explored further. It is almost certain that some types of better-quality chert were imported from elsewhere. Only 4% of the flaked assemblage was produced from imported beach flint. Local sandstones and other coarse stone materials were used for macro-tools such as the polished stone axeheads, quern-stones and rubbing stones. It is important to note that over 50% of stone tools were recovered from the infill layers, which are thought to derive from the top of the mound (Kelleher, in prep.; pers. comm.).

The flaked assemblage component contains only five single-platform cores (nodules of raw material with one flat platform from which flakes and blades are removed), which is unusual and suggests that initial knapping may have taken place elsewhere on better-quality chert. The majority of cores were produced on flakes that were reduced using a previously unrecognised controlled bipolar-on-an-anvil technique on low- to medium-quality local chert nodules (see Illus. 8). This type of technology involves the use of an anvil upon which

Creative Minds

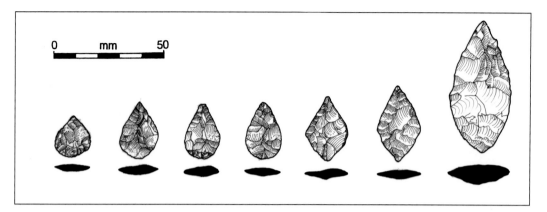

Illus. 4—Six of the nine miniature leaf-shaped arrowheads from Tullahedy (Patsi Bates).

the core, often a flake itself, would be placed and held at a suitable angle during flake detachment, hence increasing the control one has over the removal process. This technology has since been identified in six other important Middle Neolithic assemblages and may be regionally confined (Sternke 2008a–d; 2009a–c). Until recently, bipolar techniques have been considered primitive and impoverished, but this view is slowly changing in the light of emerging evidence to the contrary. The modified tools include hide-scrapers, plano-convex knives and various other forms. There is ample evidence for intense arrowhead production at this site. Eighty finished, broken and preformed (unfinished) arrowheads, predominantly of the leaf- or lozenge-shaped type, were identified in the assemblage. This includes a rather enigmatic group of nine miniature leaf-shaped examples (Illus. 4).

The 137 axeheads and axehead fragments (Illus. 5 & 6) recovered at Tullahedy were produced on different raw materials, including sandstone, chert, siltstone, volcanic tuff, porcellanite, gabbro etc. (see Beese, in prep., for a detailed report).

Arrowhead manufacture

Illustration 7 shows what is considered to be the standard way of producing an arrowhead from a flat round nodule. The technique of pressure flaking with a pointed piece of bone or antler is used to thin and shape the arrowhead during the final stage of production. Most of the by-products shown in Illus. 7 are present at Tullahedy, but the use of a different raw material, namely chert, brings with it its own set of challenges. Because chert is only available in blocks or subangular nodules, it is impossible to shape it into an arrowhead without splitting it into one or several flakes. Each individual flake can then become the equivalent of the cobble shown in Illus. 7. While this is the standard way of producing an arrowhead, it is by no means the only option.

Illustration 8 demonstrates what most likely also happened at Tullahedy. Many of the available subangular nodules of chert could not be turned into single-platform cores, owing to their shape and often inferior quality. They could, however, be reduced using the bipolar method (Illus. 8) and thinned to a level where it was then possible to apply pressure retouch. During recent fieldwork carried out at HAF Lejre (the Historical and Archaeological Research Centre) in Denmark, North American flint-knapper Steve Watts, who is highly experienced in producing a variety of arrowhead forms, was given the task of producing an

From boy to man: 'rights' of passage and the lithic assemblage from Tullahedy, Co. Tipperary

Illus. 5—Polished stone axeheads produced from local raw materials (Tomas Tyner).

Illus. 6—Polished stone axeheads produced from exotic raw materials (Tomas Tyner).

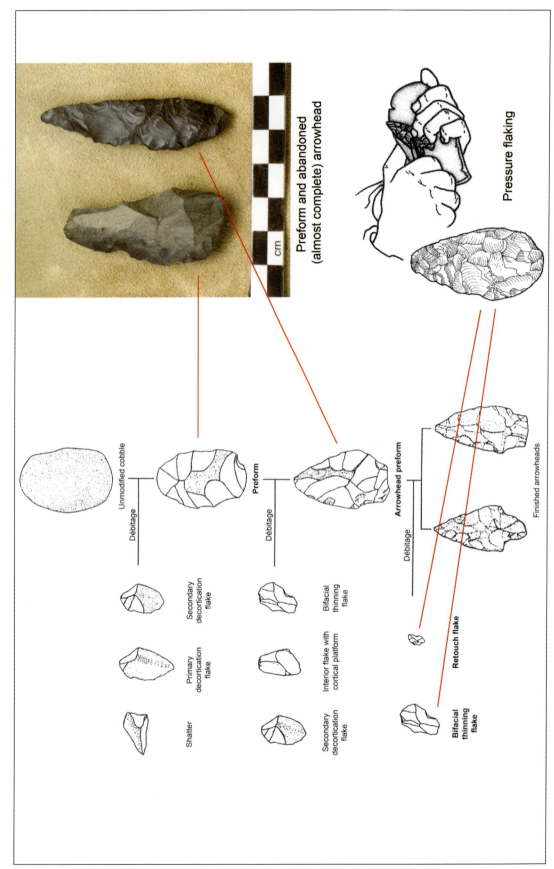

Illus. 7—*Conventional arrowhead production at Tullahedy (after Nassaney 1996; photo by Farina Sternke; drawings by Alan Brady (knapping) and Patsi Bates (arrowhead)).*

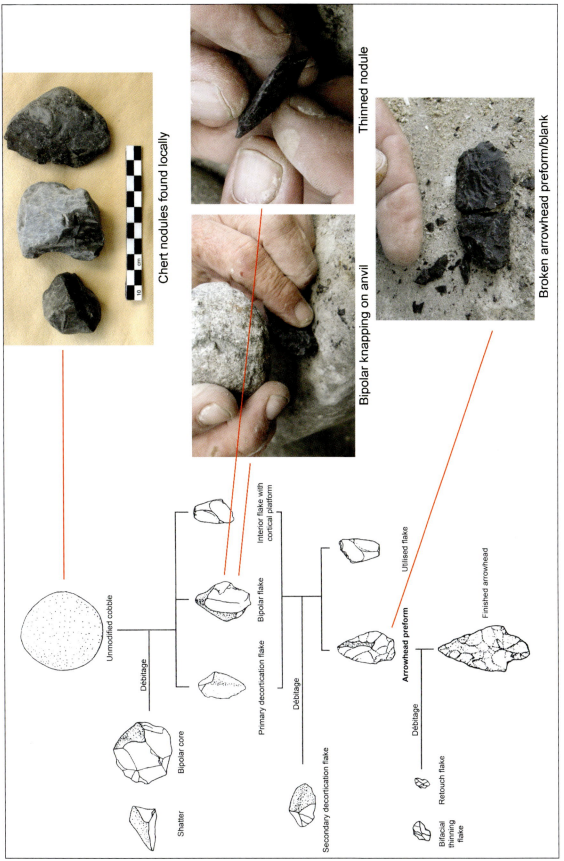

Illus. 8—*Bipolar arrowhead production at Tullahedy (after Nassaney 1996; photos by Farina Sternke).*

arrowhead from one or all of the chert nodules shown in Illus. 7. He was not at all convinced that this task was possible and complained about the size, shape and quality of the raw material provided by the author. Steve was ready to give up after just three minutes, when it was suggested that he might try the bipolar method, which worked extremely well until the preformed arrowhead broke in half (Illus. 8). Nevertheless, the resulting very thin preform could easily be turned into a miniature arrowhead of the type found at Tullahedy.

Given that the use of the bipolar technology is so dominant at Tullahedy, it is highly likely that this method was also used to thin the available nodules for arrowhead production. At least one example has been identified in the assemblage so far, but this method would certainly not have been regarded as the norm and was perhaps used by less skilled or apprentice knappers (see below).

Polished stone axehead manufacture

In comparison, the manufacture of polished stone axeheads is a straightforward process involving the selection of a suitably shaped, flattish nodule of raw material, which is then shaped into a preform through flaking and ground using sand, water and a slab of sandstone. Such grinding stones do exist in the archaeological record and at least two examples were recovered at Tullahedy. The axehead is then hafted and ready to be used. An axehead would have been re-sharpened and in some instances also reworked many times throughout its use life.

Most of the 137 axeheads and axehead fragments recovered at Tullahedy were produced locally on inferior-quality chert, sandstone and siltstone nodules and cobbles, but the best and largest examples (Illus. 6) are made of non-local and even exotic raw materials such as dolerite and gabbro (Beese, in prep.). These high-quality axeheads were made at specialised manufacturing centres elsewhere. Some of these exotic specimens, if not all, reached Tullahedy in the form of rough-outs and were ground and polished on the site alongside the inferior, locally produced axeheads. The trading of roughed-out (pre-shaped) axeheads is very common throughout the Neolithic period in Ireland and elsewhere in Europe.

Ethnographic examples of apprenticeships in stone-working

Prehistoric children would have been aware of stonecraft and other manufacturing processes from a very young age through sound, vision and smell. They would later play with stone and stone implements and imitate the actions and movements of adults carrying out daily tasks involving stone tools. Children would also routinely participate in these tasks by helping out and getting involved in some stages of the production processes, for example carrying raw material, prior to entering a formal apprenticeship (see Lancy 2008 for specific ethnographic examples of child labour). Many archaeologists, however, believe that stonecraft, and particularly specialised activities such as arrowhead and stone axehead manufacture, can only be acquired through teaching and continuous practice; a formal apprenticeship is often envisaged. Such apprenticeships are known from specific ethnographic examples—for instance, polished stone axehead manufacture in Papua New Guinea (Stout 2002; Sillitoe 2004) and Harrapan stone bead manufacture in India (Roux et al. 1995; Roux & Blascó 2000). Here, children generally enter into an apprenticeship at the age of 10–12 years and remain apprentices for at least seven years (Pétrequin & Pétrequin 1993; Roux et al. 1995; Stout 2002).

Several archaeological and historical examples of participation in peripheral activities and gradual integration into the production process prior to a more formal apprenticeship exist, particularly in relation to arrowhead, axehead, dagger and gunflint manufacture (Sternke 2001; Apel 2001; 2008; Baxter 2005; Stout 2002; Sillitoe 2004; Whittaker 2001). A Danish Mesolithic example involved the production of so-called transverse arrowheads (Sternke 2001; 2005; Sternke & Sørensen 2009). The existence of a small number of atypical arrowheads at this site in Sparrgård, Falster, suggests a gradual integration into the production process prior to a more formal apprenticeship. Here, beginner or novice knappers manufactured arrowheads from blanks produced by a skilled knapper. The question of whether these arrowheads were actually used by adults for hunting or merely represent children's play remains to be answered in future research. In any case, it is important to note that the nature and organisation of 'apprenticeship' is highly dependent on the availability of raw material (Ferguson 2003; 2008; Sternke, in prep. b), which can also influence the degree to which children are involved in and contribute to day-to-day lithic production.

Apprenticeship and the Tullahedy assemblage

Evidence of artefacts and production processes that deviate from the generally accepted norm are plentiful at Tullahedy. While some of these artefacts and processes such as the bipolar knapping can be viewed as innovation, imitation and evidence for apprenticeship, others solely belong to the class of apprentices' products—for example, the many abandoned arrowhead preforms and arrowhead fragments which are the result of failed productions (Illus. 9).

Similar failed production attempts can be observed within the group of locally produced

Illus. 9—Failed arrowhead productions (Farina Sternke).

Creative Minds

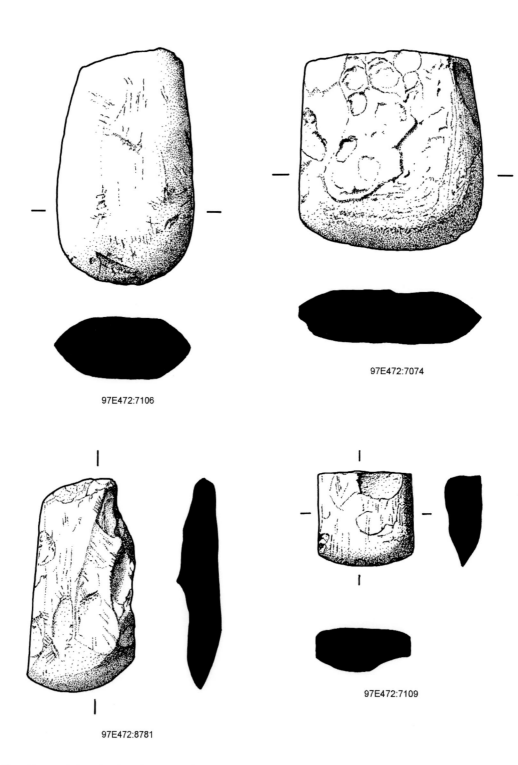

Illus. 10—Failed axehead productions; scale 1:1 (Patsi Bates).

stone axeheads (Illus. 5 & 10). In fact, everything about them appears to be wrong: the raw material is unsuitable, the workmanship is poor and they were certainly not functional. Many of them would have broken during the first few minutes of use. Their manufacture, however, provided an excellent opportunity for practice. The broken and failed axeheads were later reused as cores for blade production, and in one instance an axehead appears to have been broken in half deliberately.

Like most of the arrowheads, 70 axeheads and axehead fragments derive from the infill layers believed to have come from the top of the mound. Whatever took place on the summit was related to the manufacture and use of stone axeheads and arrowheads and was probably considered very important by the inhabitants of this site. It is possible that the summit was used for ritual ceremonies (see Whittle 1997 for a discussion of the importance of the man-made Silbury Hill, Wiltshire, England), perhaps related to, among other things, rites of passage. It may well have been the location where the transfer of knowledge associated with apprenticeships took place and where adolescents were subjected to, participated in and passed through various rites of passage on the way to adulthood. To pass through the rites did not merely mean that one was considered an adult but also that one had acquired the right to participate fully in society, to shape it and to contribute to its physical, economic and social reproduction. What remains to be explored in the future is whether such rites of passage were clearly divided along gender lines, as is the case in about half of the world's indigenous populations (Lancy & Grove, in press; Schlegel & Barry 1980).

Overall interpretation of the arrowhead and polished axehead production

The excavator has previously suggested that the Tullahedy mound encompasses a probable enclosed Neolithic ritual complex with associated domestic activity (Kelleher, in prep.; pers. comm.). Towards the end of the Neolithic period, soil and lithic material were cleared from the summit and deposited to build up the sides of the mound and level the surrounding topography (see Whittle 1997 for a similar phenomenon at Silbury Hill). The lithic analysis has identified abundant evidence of specialised on-site arrowhead production. The flake blanks for the largest and most skilfully produced arrowheads were produced elsewhere by expert knappers on good-quality chert, perhaps at an unidentified quarry site or river bank. In this respect, the almost complete absence of flint in the assemblage is remarkable. Despite the fact that the site is located far inland, it was normal practice in the Neolithic to import flint from the beaches in the form of pre-prepared nodules, blanks or even finished tools. There is very little evidence of this at Tullahedy. Instead, local chert nodules and flakes were exploited, using the bipolar-on-an-anvil technique.

In contrast to the on-site arrowhead production, specialised, high-quality axehead production took place elsewhere. This comprised axeheads produced on volcanic and other exotic rock types. The locally produced axeheads exhibit little skill and are made of unsuitable, poor-quality chert, sandstone and siltstone. From this it can be inferred that most of the on-site knapping was carried out by novices and beginners on local, inferior-quality raw materials, which possibly derived from glacial till, local outcrops and river beds. Much of this knapping appears to have been carried out on the summit of the mound and was most likely linked to formal apprenticeships, and perhaps also to ritual activities associated with rites of passage. Chert must have been integral to these activities, as well as to the overall status of this site and to the identity formation of the inhabitants, who wished to connect with and transform their local environment.

Conclusion

The mound at Tullahedy is special in many ways. The manipulation of the local landscape through the transformation of the mound and the special role that was afforded to the arrowheads and polished stone axeheads produced on locally sourced raw materials point towards a use of the site as a ritual centre with important social activities taking place on the summit.

As significant as the Neolithic mound at Tullahedy is, it is not entirely unique. At least three similar high-status Neolithic sites (Feltrim Hill, Co. Dublin, Lyles Hill, Co. Antrim, and Donegore Hill, Co. Antrim) with large collections of axeheads and arrowheads are known (Hartnett & Eogan 1964; Evans 1953; Mallory & Hartwell 1984). None of these, however, have yet been linked to settlement sites. The only other similar site in that respect is the Knockadoon complex at Lough Gur, Co. Limerick (Ó Ríordáin 1954; Woodman & Scannell 1993), but even there the differences, when looked at more closely, are greater than the similarities. The use and transformation of the mound at Tullahedy may represent important social shifts in landscape perception, and may also have been central to identity formation both of and within prehistoric societies in this region. Such shifts can only be identified because diverse raw materials were exploited differently and with varying intensities. It is important to realise that research that focuses exclusively on the study of flint is unlikely to recognise this. In this respect alone, the Neolithic mound at Tullahedy and its remarkable assemblage offer a valuable lesson. It is to be hoped that future research will answer some of the many remaining questions about this site and its artefact assemblages.

Acknowledgements

I am grateful to the NRA for providing the opportunity to publish this paper, and to the Department of Archaeology, UCC, Hilary Kelleher and Rose Cleary for allowing me to study the assemblage. Thanks also to Steve Watts for his assistance with the experimental knapping and to Anthony Beese for his geological identifications and geological background information.

Notes

1. NGR 183440, 177220; height 50–55 m OD; excavation reg. no. E0427; ministerial direction no. A26; SMR no. TN020-079002.
2. Excavation licence no. 97E0472; excavation director Cia McConway.

2. Spindle-whorls and hand-spinning in Ireland
Richard O'Brien

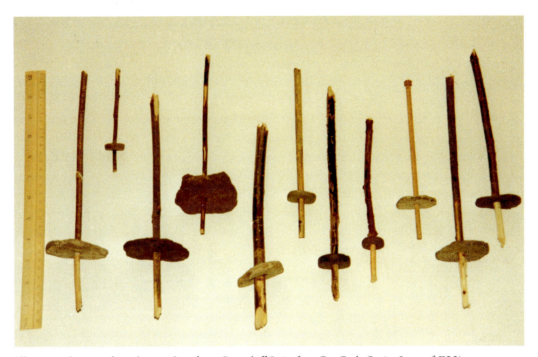

Illus. 1—Eleven perforated stone discs from Garryduff I ringfort, Co. Cork (Janice Long of F22).

Hand-spinning of fibres was the only method of making yarn to weave into clothing until the invention of the spinning-wheel in the medieval period. Spinning undoubtedly evolved from hand-twisting fibres for basketry and ropes, where the twisting provided natural tension and strength. The earliest woven cloth found to date consists of flax thread recently identified in soil samples from a cave in Georgia and dated to 34,000 years ago (Durrani 2010, 10).

Hand-spinning thread entailed the use of a rod of wood or bone known as a spindle. The spindle had a notch in the top or bottom to draw out natural fibres, and a long narrow body around which the thread was wound when spun. In Europe hand-spinning was generally carried out using the suspended spindle method, with the spindle weighted at one end with a centrally perforated object known as a spindle-whorl (Illus. 1). This gave momentum to the rotation of the spindle and also provided balance and equilibrium during spinning. The position of the whorl on the spindle, at the top, middle or bottom, was either culturally determined or dependent on the spinner's own preference. The length of the spindle varied depending on whorl size, the type of fibre being spun and the preference of the spinner.

Thread and woven cloth rarely survive in archaeological contexts unless the right environmental conditions exist, but spindle-whorls commonly do survive and provide valuable evidence for the spinning of thread. One of the earliest published Irish examples was a whorl still attached low on a wooden spindle found in Moylarg crannog, Co. Antrim (Buick 1893, 34).

On a worldwide basis, there is evidence for a wide variety of hand-spinning techniques: without a spindle; with spindle only or using a hooked stick (no whorl); using multiple whorls on a spindle; rotating the spindle in the hand with or without a whorl; grasping the spindle (with whorl); supporting the spindle (with whorl), with the spindle resting on the thigh or standing upright in a bowl or cup; and, the commonest form, the suspended spindle method (Crowfoot 1931, 7–11; Nyberg 1990, 78–81).

Many fibres can be spun into yarn: vegetable and fruit fibres like cotton, silk, jute, sisal, ramie, hemp and nettle, and animal fibres from the horse, cow, goat, camel, musk, llama, alpaca, dog and even cat (Chadwick 1989, 100–26). In Ireland wool and flax were the main sources for cloth-making; some fibres from the above list were undoubtedly also used as raw materials for yarn, although there is no surviving evidence for this. There is no evidence for wool production prior to the Late Bronze Age (McCormack & Murray 2007, 26), but flax seeds have been recorded from the Early Bronze Age, with impressed seeds on a tripartite bowl from Aghfarrell, Co. Dublin (Henshall 1950, 140; M McClatchie, pers. comm.). Recently, seven flax seeds were found along with sherds of Early Bronze Age funerary pottery in the upper fill of a cremation pit in Barnagore 4, Co. Cork, the lower fill of which dated from 2300–2040 BC (Danaher 2004, 24). To spin fibres from flax stems a distaff (a rod on which the flax was wound preparatory to spinning) would have been used, as it helped to keep the fibres untangled. A number of wooden objects first classified as spindles from Ballinderry No. 2, Co. Offaly (Hencken 1942), and Lagore, Co. Meath (Hencken 1950), may have been a type of distaff (Patterson 1956, 82).

At present there are a number of well-known Irish examples of prehistoric textiles, all dating from within the Late Bronze Age (1100–800 BC). The most famous is a plain-weave woollen cloth and black horsehair belt tassel from Armoy, Co. Antrim (Henshall 1950, 134–8). A fragment of woollen fabric of fine to medium fibre was found (with spindle-whorls) at Island MacHugh, Co. Tyrone (ibid., 138; Davies 1950, 36). A more recent example was the recovery of textiles from a bog in Killymoon Demesne, Co. Tyrone (Hurl 1996). Analysis has revealed seven pieces of cloth (two of wool, five of bast fibre/linen[?]), two pieces of wool cord and locks of animal and human hair (Heckett 2007). The discovery of these early textiles is generally attributable to their survival in wetland contexts. There are many examples of textiles from early medieval and medieval sites in Ireland (Heckett 1991).

As hand-spinning was such an integral part of everyday life, many materials were used by the spinner to make whorls. Materials as diverse as the ends of human thigh bones, lead, wood, animal bone, antler, ivory, clay, broken pottery, jet, amber, bronze, iron, stone (generally sandstone but occasionally mudstone, limestone, slate and steatite), glass, coal and even dried cow-dung have been recorded. Once roughly shaped and perforated centrally, a whorl could be created from almost anything. Antiquary Sir Arthur Mitchell recorded an encounter in Inverness-shire in 1866 with an elderly Scottish woman who was spinning with a potato, having used nothing else all her life (Knowles 1905, 6). Whorls were also used in necklaces; the same object served a dual purpose (Illus. 2). Since hand-spinning was a mobile rather than an exclusively indoor activity, whorls can be found anywhere on an archaeological site, and very often occur as stray finds.

In Ireland there was less variety in whorl types, with stone being the most common. Wooden whorls are rare but the early medieval royal site of Lagore crannog produced a

Illus. 2—Modern-day clay whorls from Plateau State, central Nigeria, used on a necklace and on a spindle (Richard O'Brien).

large, perforated hazel disc that was catalogued as a possible whorl (Hencken 1950, 162, fig. 82 [W98]). Bone disc-shaped whorls are rare, with single examples recorded from Ballinderry No. 2 (Hencken 1942, 54–5, fig. 22), Lagore (Hencken 1950, 194, fig. 106), Freestone Hill, Co. Kilkenny (Raftery 1969, 24, fig. 13), and Garryduff I, Co. Cork (O'Kelly 1962, 66–7, fig. 2). Occasionally other materials were used, such as a possible lead whorl from Clough Castle motte and bailey, Co. Down (Waterman 1954, 145, fig. 14), and a jet whorl from Ballyfounder rath, Co. Down (Waterman 1958, 50, fig. 8).

How to identify a spindle-whorl

Based on the findings from an MA research thesis (O'Brien 1993) that involved the examination of perforated and unperforated Irish discs, coupled with experimentation of hand-spinning with perforated objects (see below) and more recent analysis of such objects from NRA-funded excavations, it is possible to suggest parameters within which whorls can be readily identified.

A primary consideration is the weight of the object, and it is essential for this to be recorded in excavation reports. Generally, the weight range should lie between 8 g and (probably not exceeding) 500 g, depending on the fibres used and the type of yarn desired (light whorls will tend to produce lighter yarns, or simply will not revolve on the spindle, negating the entire purpose). Studies of Viking whorls from Birka, Sweden, found that whorls weighing under 10 g could not have been used for anything other than the production of very thin linen or wool (Andersson 2007, 150).

With regard to size, a diameter range of 34–134 mm is common, with most whorls measuring less than 70 mm. At Danebury hillfort in England, for example, whorl limits at 100 mm in size and 300 g in weight have been proposed, beyond which other functions should be attributed to the objects (Cunliffe 1984, 8). A diameter of less than 30 mm was probably too small to have allowed the object to keep rotating during spinning unless it was considerably thick and provided sufficient weight. A thickness range of 3–25 mm is acceptable but uniform thickness is not necessary. The thicker the whorl at the centre, the better the grip on the spindle, making spinning movements smoother.

The overall shape should be generally circular to aid the rotation on the spindle, but as long as there is sufficient balance a perfect circular shape is not necessary. The sectional profile largely depends on the material used; stone is generally disc-shaped, bone is hemispherical. A central or almost central perforation with a profile not overly slanted and a perforation size of 7–34 mm in diameter is ideal. A perforation of less than 4 mm is probably too narrow to have gripped the spindle sufficiently and such perforated objects may be more correctly classified as beads. Too large a perforation relative to overall size results in using a thicker spindle, contributing less weight where it is needed most, negating the entire purpose. Such perforated objects may be classified as net/line-sinkers or loom-weights.

Decoration alone should not be used to date whorls, as the common concentric circles were the simplest and most obvious way to decorate such objects; examples are found from the Bronze Age right through to the medieval era. The bowl-shaped examples from Cahercommaun stone fort, Co. Clare (Hencken 1938), include perfectly concentric circles with ring-and-dot motifs but these are rarities. Type and degree of decoration probably depended on the spinner's preference, so variation is to be expected.

Dating of Irish whorls

Prehistory

Prehistoric whorls are rare, most likely because the raw materials used to make them were organic and generally do not survive. It is conceivable that once farming was well established Late Neolithic people spun fibres into thread, and Henshall (1950, 132) states that in the British Early Bronze Age spinning was remarkably fine. A potential early whorl is recorded from Ballyalton court tomb, Co. Down. This disc-shaped perforated stone was found with a hoard of 44 flints at the side of an orthostat socket (Evans & Davies 1934, 101; Herity 1987, 206, 209, fig. 37). As its weight is unrecorded its classification as a whorl is uncertain, but Henshall (1950, 142) identified it as a likely Neolithic whorl.

Perforated objects from prehistoric sites such as Site F and Circles J, K and L at Knockadoon, Lough Gur, Co. Limerick (Ó Ríordáin 1954, fig. 47; Grogan & Eogan 1987, figs 13, 20 and 37), and Labbacallee wedge tomb, Co. Cork (Leask & Price 1936, fig. 4), either defined solely as beads or not considered as whorls on account of being too light/heavy (even though no weight was provided) or too irregular, should be reassessed. Another possible stone whorl was recovered from the base of a disturbed cairn of an Early Bronze Age wedge tomb at Baurnadomeeny, Co. Tipperary (O'Kelly 1960, 104, fig. 4). The excavator favoured a bead function for this object but as no weight was given in the report the whorl function should not be discounted.

The increase in the discovery of prehistoric sites over the last two decades has led to the finding of more Bronze Age whorls. A potential Early Bronze Age disc-shaped whorl was found in the primary fill of an as yet undated cremation burial from Rath-Healy 1, Co. Cork (Linnane 2006, 35, pl. 28). If this pit is a bona fide cremation burial, and the whorl is not a later, intrusive find, this would be the earliest instance of a whorl buried as a grave-good.

Other stone disc-shaped whorls found in association with houses and in other domestic contexts include a highly decorated whorl from a subcircular structure at Killemly, Co. Tipperary (Illus. 3), firmly dated to the Middle Bronze Age (1256–1012 BC). This is currently the earliest example of a whorl decorated with a motif of multiple concentric lines (O'Brien 2009a). A similar, although undecorated, stone whorl was found at a Late Bronze Age site at Ballyveelish, Co. Tipperary (Doody 1987, 25, fig. 2:4). A siltstone whorl decorated with a single concentric line on each face was found in a burnt mound/*fulacht*

Illus. 3—Middle Bronze Age stone whorl from Killemly, Co. Tipperary. This is the earliest recorded Irish example of a whorl decorated with three concentric lines (John Sunderland).

fiadh trough at Coarhamore, Co. Kerry (Sheehan 1990, 35). Although first thought to be early medieval in date, largely based on decoration, this whorl can now be firmly dated to the Late Bronze Age (O'Brien 1993, 138).

An undecorated disc-shaped stone whorl weighing 50 g from a Late Bronze Age roundhouse in Tober, Co. Offaly, represents one of the heaviest prehistoric whorls found to date (O'Brien 2009b; Walsh 2007, 15). Three potential Late Bronze Age whorls (two bone hemispherical types and one disc-shaped stone whorl) were found at Ballinderry No. 2 crannog (Hencken 1942, 9, fig. 6), and three bone whorls (two hemispherical and one bowl-shaped) were recovered from the hillfort of Freestone Hill, Co. Kilkenny (Raftery 1969, 61). If these bone examples are definitively Late Bronze Age they are the earliest of this whorl type in Ireland.

The largest collection of prehistoric whorls was recovered from a remarkable Late Bronze Age site at Killymoon Demesne, Co. Tyrone, dated to 1100–800 BC. Ten stone whorls (both complete and incomplete) plus two stone disc rough-outs were found in association with textiles, gold objects, saddle querns, a bronze axe and coarse pottery (Hurl 1996; pers. comm.; Heckett 2007, 29, 32, fig. 2, table 1).

Medieval period
It is from the early medieval period that the vast majority of whorls survive, with important assemblages from ringforts such as Garryduff I (O'Kelly 1962) and Lisleagh I (Monk 1995) in County Cork, and Lagore crannog. Recently published examples include a possible lathe-turned decorated antler whorl and a disc-shaped stone example, both from an enclosure site at Killickaweeny 1, Co. Kildare, dated to between the eighth and 10th centuries (Walsh 2008, 48, fig. 3.10).

Significant Viking whorl assemblages have been recovered from urban excavations, particularly in Dublin City (Ó Ríordáin 1971; Wallace 1985); the analysis of these whorls would allow comparisons with whorl collections from the Viking homelands. A number of lead whorls (often confused with perforated lead pan weights) were recorded from a rural settlement at Woodstown, Co. Waterford (O'Brien 2004; O'Brien & Russell 2005). A catalogue of six of the major published assemblages of whorls and spindles from a variety of international Viking-period excavations by Priest-Dorman (2000), who analysed 1,356 whorls and 46 spindles, suggested a statistical ratio of the occurrence of one spindle to every 29 whorls. This factor may explain the paucity of spindles, and indeed distaffs, on excavations in Ireland.

With the introduction of the spinning-wheel in the late medieval period hand-spinning was replaced, although, as we have seen in the Scottish tale recounted above, the fondness for the old method of spinning undoubtedly persisted into the post-medieval period in some areas.

There is also documentary evidence for hand-spinning and weaving in early medieval Irish society. For instance, the law-text *Cáin Lánamna* mentions divisions of wool (sheared, combed and greased for both yarn and cloth) with reference to divorce laws (Binchy 1978, 56; Kelly 1998, 269–70). The division and designation of those who undertook spinning and weaving are also documented; evidently it was perceived as women's work to spin and weave, but Kelly (ibid., 452) also relates that boys of commoner rank were taught how to comb wool. Undoubtedly younger children watched their mothers spinning and weaving and would have learned to play with spindles as 'spinning-tops' when they got the chance.

In Irish folklore there was a tradition of tying a whorl to a cow's tale to improve milk yield and the objects were sometimes known as 'fairy millstones' (Prim 1855, 399).

Whorl typologies

Whorls (intact and incomplete) are a frequent find on excavations but rarely in any great numbers (apart from some sites subject to almost 100% excavation, such as Cahercommaun and Garryduff I). Whether this is attributable to specialisation (centres of whorl production/use), differential preservation or the spinner retaining her favourite whorl from site to site is difficult to determine. Whorls can be found on a variety of site types and in numerous contexts.

One of the earliest Irish publications on whorls, by Knowles (1905), was a descriptive account of those from his own extensive collection. Hencken (1938, 43, fig. 27) produced the first scientific typology of whorls based on bone and stone examples recovered from his excavations at Cahercommaun. His typology classified whorls on the basis of shape (hemispherical, cylindrical, bowl- and disc-shaped) and on the degree of modification and finish. Whorls made from the heads of ox thigh bones were represented in all four types and were decorated profusely with concentric lines and/or dots, while the stone whorls were all disc-shaped. Hencken's classification is useful but has no bearing on the suitability of these objects as whorls, being concerned solely with their finished appearance.

Stone discs (complete/incomplete, partly perforated/unperforated) have often been found on archaeological sites dating from the Bronze Age onwards (Hurl 1996; O'Kelly 1951, 84). Garryduff I ringfort produced 98 stone discs (Illus. 4), the largest collection in

Illus. 4—Selection of stone whorls and stone disc rough-outs from Garryduff I ringfort, Co. Cork (Janice Long of F22).

Ireland, of which 86 were unperforated (O'Brien 1993, 145). Interpretation of function can vary widely, depending on disc size and weight, but the whorl rough-out function is often proposed (Ó Ríordáin 1942, 111; O'Kelly 1962, 91). Of the 20 stone discs from the monastic site of Reask, Co. Kerry, 15 plano-convex examples were known locally as *caidhti* (quoits) and were used to play a game of the same name (Fanning 1981, 129).

Experimenting with whorls

As a whorl helped to give the spindle momentum during spinning, knowing the object's size and weight is crucial. In England experimental hand-spinning on objects from Northampton found that whorls weighing over 40 g may have been used for plying two or more yarns (Oakley & Hall 1979, 286–7), although Walton Rogers (1997, 1745) cautions against assigning definitive whorl weights to types of yarn. Some of the earliest experimental work in Ireland was conducted in the 1950s when Patterson (1956, 81) showed that a spindle from Lough Faughan, Co. Down, was more likely to have been a distaff.

As part of a Master's degree the author commissioned an experienced hand-spinner, Theresa Diane Mullins, to experiment with perforated stones from the Lisleagh I and Garryduff I ringforts (Illus. 5–6). The spinner used newly shorn Suffolk Down fleece, with spindles of fresh hazel and willow (seasoned wood was unreliable as it cracked easily during spinning). These spindles needed to be stored away from direct sunlight to prevent them from drying out, which tended to loosen the whorl when attached. A carpenter lathe-turned a number of pine spindles based on examples found at Ballinderry No. 2 crannog;

Illus. 5—Tying the leader threads to the top of the spindle before the fibres are spun (whorl no. 29 from Garryduff I, weight 96.7 g) (Richard O'Brien).

Illus. 6—Passing the fibres through the fingers as the spindle rotates freely (whorl no. 29 from Garryduff I) (Richard O'Brien).

pine was used as he found that softer woods tended to break on the lathe.

The spinner carefully selected the most appropriate spindle to fit each object. A larger spindle was specifically designed to spin with a very heavy disc (430.2 g and 128.8–134 mm diameter) from Lisleagh I, with favourable results as the spinner found that the large spindle improved control during spinning. Such a heavy disc would normally be classified as a loom-weight but the experimental work proved that it worked perfectly as a whorl (Illus. 7–8). Wool was sorted and teased (dirt and knots removed) for between half an hour and one hour for each experiment, so preparing a mass of wool first was more efficient. The spinner used the suspended spindle method with the whorl low on the spindle at all times.

Once prepared, a clump of wool was twisted between the fingers (teasing) continually in the same direction until a length of yarn was produced. This length (the leader) was then knotted onto the spindle beneath the whorl, carried around the whorl and attached again to the top of the spindle, leaving a short length of yarn protruding. More wool was then teased and attached to the length of yarn (already produced) and with a short twist of the fingers the spindle free-falls, rotating in one direction only, while the spinner teases more wool. The spindle stops rotating when it reaches the ground and, before any backward movement occurs (which could untangle the threads), the spinner gathers the spun yarn and attaches it around the whorl, and so on until a cone of spun yarn has been produced. Yarns have either an S-twist

Illus. 7—Spinning with the heavy stone whorl from Lisleagh I, using the lathe-turned pine spindle (whorl no. 11, weight 430.2 g) (Richard O'Brien).

Illus. 8—The Lisleagh I heavy whorl during rotation: the spinner found this whorl excellent to use on this spindle (Richard O'Brien).

or a Z-twist, depending on the direction of spinning. The yarn is then ready to be woven into cloth.

The author himself also experimented with undated perforated bone objects found at Dún Aonghasa, Inis Mór, Co. Galway (Cotter 1996). Suffolk Down wool and spindles of hazel and willow (165–243 mm in length) were used, with the whorl low on the spindle. Spinning time varied between whorls, but within one hour a couple of metres of yarn was produced from each test; the threads varied in thickness (0.25–3 mm) and ranged from 22 to 28 tpi (threads/twists per inch, indicating the tightness of twist produced). The coarsest and most irregular thread was produced from a damaged whorl, which might have been rectified by an experienced spinner; the other bone objects worked sufficiently well.

The experiments using both the stone and bone objects can be used to suggest limits on the size, shape and weight of whorls (Illus. 9), bearing in mind that these experiments

Illus. 9 (left)—This stone whorl (Lisleagh I whorl no. 201, weight 7.8 g) was too light and lacked momentum during rotation, causing the spindle to hit the spinner's leg (Richard O'Brien).

Illus. 10 (above)—Examples of the spun yarn from the experimental hand-spinning using the Lisleagh I stone whorls (Richard O'Brien).

only used wool and that other fibres may show different results. The experiments proved that even irregularly shaped rough discs can function perfectly on a spindle (Illus. 10).

Conclusion

It is hoped that this brief introduction to hand-spinning and whorls in Ireland will lead to a reassessment of earlier whorl assemblages, particularly those from prehistoric sites. Fundamentally, when describing whorls in excavation reports the weight must be provided: without this basic knowledge, defining perforated objects will remain problematic. A realisation of the potential wide range of raw materials for both whorl production and spinning, as well as the use of literary sources, should enliven a previously narrow view of this basic but very necessary daily chore.

Acknowledgements

Thanks to NRA Archaeologist Ken Hanley for the Barnagore 4 reference, to Clare Cotter (Discovery Programme) for permission to use the Dún Aonghasa data and to Dr Meriel McClatchie for information on the flax seeds from Aghfarrell.

3. Clay and fire: the development and distribution of pottery traditions in prehistoric Ireland
Eoin Grogan and Helen Roche

Pottery forms the most informative and commonplace component of the material culture of the prehistoric period. It is durable and the typological and chronological sequence is well understood. Most pottery was functional and intended for domestic use in cooking or storage. The role of the material could be altered, however, through use in different situations: some domestic vessels became grave-offerings or were used in ceremonial contexts. In certain periods, for example the Early Bronze Age (2200–1600 BC), highly decorated vessels were specifically created as grave-goods. Throughout prehistory it appears that potting was carried out by particularly adept individuals within each family or community, although during some periods there may have been specialist potters producing the more accomplished vessels. The primary material, the clay, appears to have been available locally, although stone inclusions may occasionally have been acquired from more distant sources.

A very large number of pottery assemblages have been recovered in the past few years as a result of excavations in advance of developments such as roads, pipelines and housing. These range from sites with fewer than 10 sherds to examples with over 10,000. While this material has been assessed within post-excavation programmes, where it often makes a significant contribution to the understanding of the site, the pace of discovery has hindered examination of the wider implications of this quantity of new information.

This paper offers a reassessment of the development sequence and chronology of prehistoric pottery types, as well as a review of the context and distribution of this material. For the Early Neolithic period (4000–3500 BC) new discoveries have indicated more widespread settlement than had previously been apparent, while at the same time highlighting areas of particular settlement concentration. Some of the new material, for example Late Neolithic (2900–2500 BC) and Chalcolithic ('Copper Age') (2500–2200 BC) pottery (Grooved Ware and Beaker, see below), has dramatically altered our understanding of the distribution of these types at both a regional and national level. (The term Chalcolithic is applied here rather than the more cumbersome, but widely accepted, 'Final Neolithic/Early Bronze Age' coined by Cooney & Grogan (1994).) The very large number of sites dating from the Middle and Late Bronze Age (1600–800 BC) suggests a significant population expansion as well as more extensive and intensive settlement during this period. Nevertheless, it is also apparent, despite the large number of new sites, that pottery production and use began to decline, leading to the abandonment of pottery at, or very soon after, the beginning of the Iron Age around 800 BC.

The Early Neolithic period (c. 4000–3500 BC)

The earliest pottery in Ireland is associated with the first farming communities and it appears that the potting techniques and vessel design were imported as a component of

Creative Minds

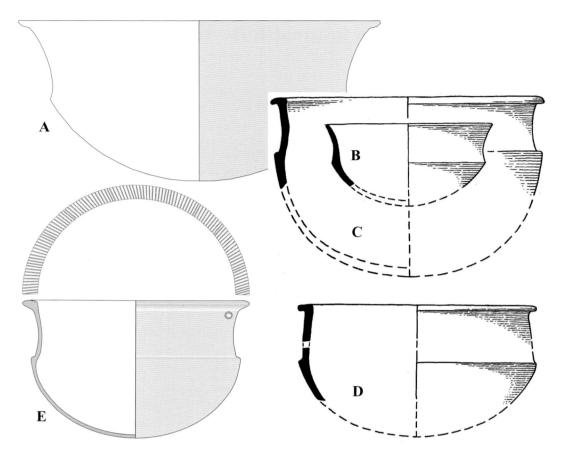

Illus. 1—Principal Early Neolithic carinated bowl forms. (A) Clontygora Large, Co. Armagh. (B–C) Lyles Hill, Co. Antrim. (D) Lough Gur, Site C, Co. Limerick. (E) Curraghprevin, Co. Cork. (A–D from Case 1961, figs 6, 8 and 10.)

agricultural traditions. The material comes principally from settlement sites, although smaller quantities have been recovered from funerary contexts, in particular court tomb deposits (Herity 1987, 149–52).

The most common form consists of carinated bowls that have rounded or beaded everted rims, upright, gently concave necks, simple angle or small step shoulders and deep, rounded body profiles (Illus. 1; Case 1961: 'Dunmurry–Ballymarlagh styles'; Sheridan 1995: 'classic carinated bowls'). These forms represent the earliest type of Neolithic pottery in Ireland and are widely dated to 4000–3500 BC. Simple hemispherical bowls at, for example, Monanny, Co. Monaghan (Walsh 2006), and Kilgobbin, Co. Dublin (Hagen 2004), are an intermittent part of the repertoire (Herity 1987, 148–9).

A developed form with expanded rims and more developed shoulders (Case 1961: 'Lyles Hill/Lough Gur Style'; Sheridan 1995: 'slightly modified carinated bowls') occurs within the extensive Lough Gur, Co. Limerick, assemblages (Ó Ríordáin 1954; Grogan & Eogan 1987). The stratigraphic evidence at Knowth, Co. Meath (Eogan 1984; Eogan & Roche 1997), where the modified vessels come from the second domestic phase, suggests a sequential development from the simpler, earlier, bowls. It has been suggested, however, that modified pottery with developed rims and shoulders could have emerged at a very early date at Donegore Hill, Co. Antrim (Mallory & Hartwell 1984; Sheridan 1995, 7).

The initial manufacturing process involved kneading the clay and adding temper and/or stone inclusions. (During the preparation of clay for making prehistoric pottery two types of material (temper and inclusions) were mixed into the natural clay to improve both firing and the quality of the pottery. Temper is organic material; this is burnt out during the firing process. Very occasionally bone or shell was used and these are resistant to fire. Inclusions are inorganic materials, generally fine particles of stone.) Limited analysis indicates that the clay was sourced locally. Quartzite, which was either crushed (giving an angular shape) or rounded (suggesting its use in a naturally rolled state), possibly derived from fine sands and gravels, is the most common inclusion but other, usually locally available, stone was also used. It appears that the clay was also folded as part of this stage, and the pottery has a characteristic striated appearance in section. Most vessels were coil-built. When the clay had dried, the surfaces were further smoothed and the exterior of the pot was burnished using a smooth stone: this produced a slightly glossy appearance after firing and may have reduced the porosity of the clay.

Distribution

Case (1961, fig. 27) documented a distribution of this pottery that was, with the exception of Lough Gur, Co. Limerick (Ó Ríordáin 1954), largely confined to north Leinster and north-east Ulster; even by the mid-1990s Sheridan's (1995) research still showed a similar restricted pattern. More recent excavations demonstrate far wider Early Neolithic settlement, while emphasising the concentration of activity in parts of the country such as Leinster and mid-Munster (Illus. 2).

The Middle Neolithic period (c. 3500–2800 BC)

This period is characterised by diversification in the pottery forms and by the application of decoration usually pressed into the pot surface using a variety of tools, including twisted and whipped cord and bone (Illus. 3). The term 'Impressed Ware' provides a useful reference for this tradition (Gibson 2002, 78–82). Important new assemblages, such as at Knockans, Rathlin Island, Co. Antrim, Balregan, Co. Louth, and Knowth, Co. Meath, have proved opportune in re-evaluating this material (Roche 2007; Grogan & Roche 2005a; Eogan & Roche 1997, 51–100: 'Decorated Pottery Complex'), while important studies include the work of Herity (1982), Case (1961) and Sheridan (1995).

The earliest forms consist of modified carinated ('bipartite') bowls with sharply in-turned necks (Illus. 3; Case 1961: 'Ballyalton bowls'; Herity 1982: 'Necked Vessels'; Sheridan 1995: 'decorated bipartite bowls'); these have a particular association with so-called 'single burials', especially those in Linkardstown tombs (Brindley & Lanting 1989/90: 'Drimnagh Style bowls'), but have also come from court tombs at Ballyedmond, Co. Down (Evans 1938), and Annaghmare, Co. Armagh (Waterman 1965), and from the portal tomb at Ballykeel, Co. Armagh (Collins 1965) (see Herity 1982, figs 47: 3, 49: 2, 31: 31). The main period for these is firmly dated to c. 3525–3350 BC (Brindley & Lanting 1989/90, 4–5, figs 1–2), but wider associations indicate that similar pottery forms may have continued later. The influence for this part of the decorative tradition comes from bipartite bowls of 'Beacharra' type, after the eponymous site in Argyll, Scotland (see Sheridan 1995, 8–11, fig. 2: 3; Herity 1982, fig. 53); vessels of this type occur at several sites in the north-east, such as

Creative Minds

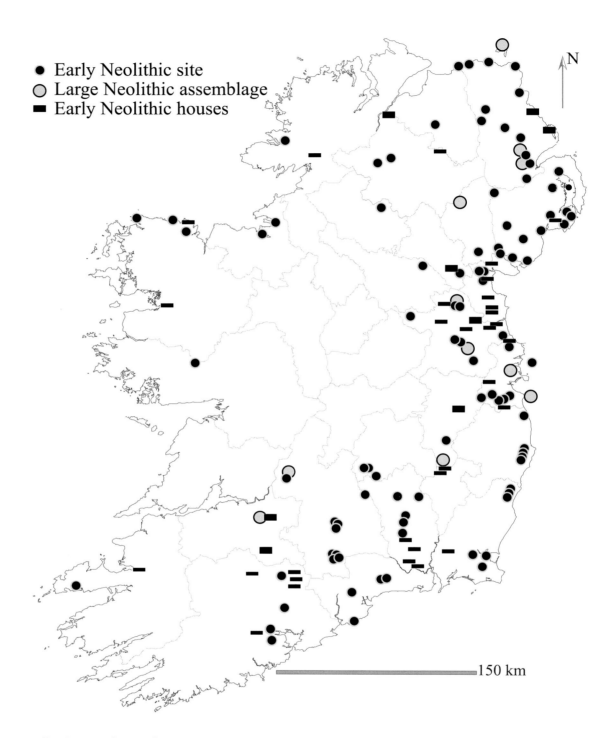

Illus. 2—Distribution of Early Neolithic carinated bowls.

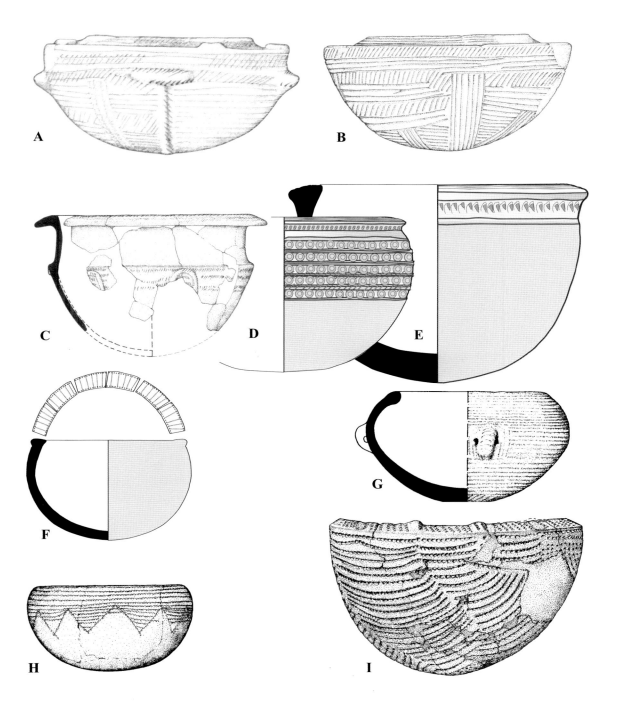

Illus. 3—Principal Middle Neolithic forms. Bipartite bowls: (A) Drimnagh, Co. Dublin; (B) Ballintruer More, Co. Wicklow. Necked vessels: (C) Lough Gur, Site C, Co. Limerick. Broad-rimmed bowls: (D) Newrath, Co. Kilkenny; (E–F) Balregan, Co. Louth. Globular bowls ('Goodland' type): (G) Rath, Co. Wicklow; (H) Tamnyrankin, Co. Derry. Globular bowls ('Carrowkeel' type): (I) Mound of the Hostages, Tara (Castleboy), Co. Meath (from O'Sullivan 2005, fig. 77). (A–C and G–H from Herity 1982, figs 22, 29, 71, 30 and 45.)

Ballymacaldrack, Ballyutoag and Carnduff, Co. Antrim (Collins 1976; Herring 1937; Piggott & Childe 1932).

Another vessel type—broad-rimmed bowls—emerges during this period. These are generally deep, hemispherical bowls with a broad flat or gently curved rim and a short, frequently constricted (cavetto) neck (Case 1961: 'Dundrum bowls'; Herity 1982: 'Broad-Rimmed Vessels'); the rim top often has a pronounced outward slope that projects over the wall. Decoration is common on the rim top but rare on the remainder of the pot. While it is found in a wide variety of contexts, most of this type of pottery has come from domestic contexts. At Linkardstown, Co. Carlow, an example was associated with a bipartite vessel (Raftery 1944; Herity 1982, fig. 18). A regional variant consisting of heavily modified carinated bowls with expanded, decorated rims and shoulders occurs principally at Lough Gur (Ó Ríordáin 1954: 'Class Ia'). A variety of simple hemispherical bowls (Case 1961: 'Sandhills Ware': 'Goodland bowls', 'Carrowkeel Ware'; Herity 1982: 'Globular bowls') dominate the final stages of the Middle Neolithic period, although a broad-rimmed bowl variant with more restrained rim expansion was also in use.

Distribution patterns

There is a major concentration in the area of north Leinster and south-east Ulster (Illus. 4). Although rarely present in large quantities, there are some important assemblages from the habitation site pre-dating the large mound in the Knowth passage tomb cemetery (Eogan & Roche 1997), the pre-tomb occupation at Townleyhall 2, Co. Louth (Eogan 1963), domestic activity at Dalkey Island and Balregan, and funerary activity at Lambay Island, Co. Dublin (Liversage 1968; Ó Donnchadha 2003; Macalister 1929). There is other occupation evidence from the Dundrum sandhills (Murlough Upper and Lower) in the area around Newcastle, Co. Down (Collins 1952; 1959), as well as late deposits in the court tombs at Ballyalton and Ballyedmond, Co. Down, and Annaghmare, Co. Armagh (Evans & Davies 1934; Evans 1938; Waterman 1965). Smaller quantities of broad-rimmed bowl also came from Newgrange, Co. Meath (Cleary 1983), and Townleyhall 1, Co. Louth (Liversage 1960).

The concentration of this material in the area from Dundrum Bay in south Down to Balregan and the Boyne Valley and the island sites at Lambay and Dalkey indicates the strength of this tradition at a regional level (Illus. 4). The interrelationships of the Impressed Ware tradition are indicated by the association of different variants: broad-rimmed bowls and both fine globular bowls of the 'Goodland' type and the coarser so-called 'Carrowkeel Ware' occur variously at Knowth, Townleyhall 2, Fourknocks 1 and 2 (Hartnett 1957; 1971) and Dalkey Island, as well as with bipartite vessels at Balregan, Ballyalton, Ballykeel, Dalkey and the Hill of Rath, Co. Louth (Duffy 2002). The recognition of 'Carrowkeel' pottery as an integral part of a broader Impressed Ware tradition is especially important as it helps to counteract a long-outdated model of passage tombs as alien or exotic within the Irish Neolithic.

At a wider level there was a significant Irish Sea context, with similar developments occurring in western Scotland from the Hebrides and Skye down to the Clyde region (Megaw & Simpson 1979, 119–26), to the Isle of Man and further south to Wales (Gibson 1995). The importance of this context has been highlighted by Sheridan (1995, 15) and Eogan & Roche (1997, 97–8), and especially by Gibson (2002, 78–82), who emphasised the widespread emergence of an Impressed Ware tradition in Ireland and Britain while noting the importance of regional variations. This aspect of regionalism has also been discussed by Cooney (2000, especially 58–60) in a wider Neolithic context.

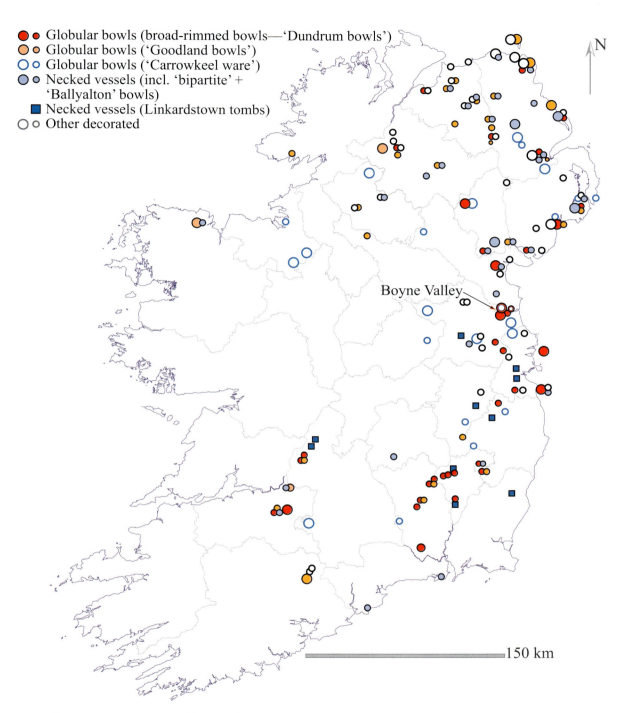

Illus. 4—Distribution of Middle Neolithic Impressed Ware.

The Late Neolithic period (c. 2850–2450 BC)

While some sporadic use of Impressed Ware, and in particular Carrowkeel Ware, is suggested, for example, by its association with a cremation at Monknewtown, Co. Meath (Sweetman 1976, 60–2, fig. 19), there is little other evidence that pottery of this tradition continued into the Late Neolithic period. The ceramic evidence is dominated by Grooved Ware (Eogan & Roche 1997; Roche 1995; Brindley 1999). These are bucket-shaped vessels with rounded, upright rims, straight or gently curved profiles and unfooted flat bases; the most common decoration consists of a characteristic groove or grooves on the inner surface immediately beneath the rim (Illus. 5). A small number with more elaborate ornament occur at Knowth and Deerpark ('Kiltierney'), Co. Fermanagh (Eogan 1984, 312, fig. 118; Brindley 1999, 32, fig. 3.4: 1), while vessels with small applied bosses came from Knowth, Longstone Cullen, Co. Tipperary, Lowpark, Co. Mayo, and Ask, Co. Wexford (Eogan & Roche 1997, pls III–IV; Roche 1996; Gillespie 2009; Gillespie & Kerrigan, forthcoming; Stevens 2007a; 2007b).

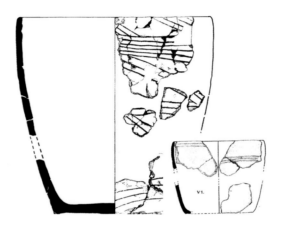

Illus. 5—Grooved Ware: Knowth, Co. Meath (from Eogan & Roche 1997).

Until recently there were only a small number of Grooved Ware sites, at Ballynahatty, Co. Down, Longstone Cullen, Kiltierney and in the Boyne Valley at Knowth and Newgrange (Hartwell 1998; Roche 1995; Eogan & Roche 1997; Cleary 1983; see also Brindley 1999, 33, fig. 3.6). Important new discoveries have been recorded at several sites, including Balgatheran and Balregan, Co. Louth, Heathstown, Rathmullan and Bettystown, Co. Meath, Lusk, Co. Dublin, and Steelstown, Co. Kildare (Ó Drisceoil 2003; Ó Donnchadha 2003; Campbell 2008; Bolger 2002; Eogan 1999; McCabe 2004; Duffy 2005). The distribution has been extended by sites at Lowpark and Kilbride, Co. Mayo (Cotter 2008), Whitewell, Co. Westmeath (Phelan 2007), Ballynacarriga, Co. Cork (Roche & Grogan 2009a; Lehane & Magee 2008; Tierney 2009), Scart, Co. Kilkenny (Monteith 2007; Laidlaw 2009), Parknahown and the Heath, Co. Laois (Grogan & Roche 2008a; Keeley 1994) (Illus. 6).

Most of the sites have evidence for timber circles or associated four-post settings. These include Ballynahatty, Knowth, Whitewell, Scart, Balgatheran, Ask, Lowpark, Kilbride and Bettystown. Apparently domestic contexts were identified at Ballynacarriga, Parknahown, Steelstown and the Heath, while at least two circular houses occur at Slieve Breagh, Co. Meath (Grogan 2004a, 111, fig. 9: 4; pottery identification by Helen Roche). Burial contexts are recorded at Knowth and Lusk.

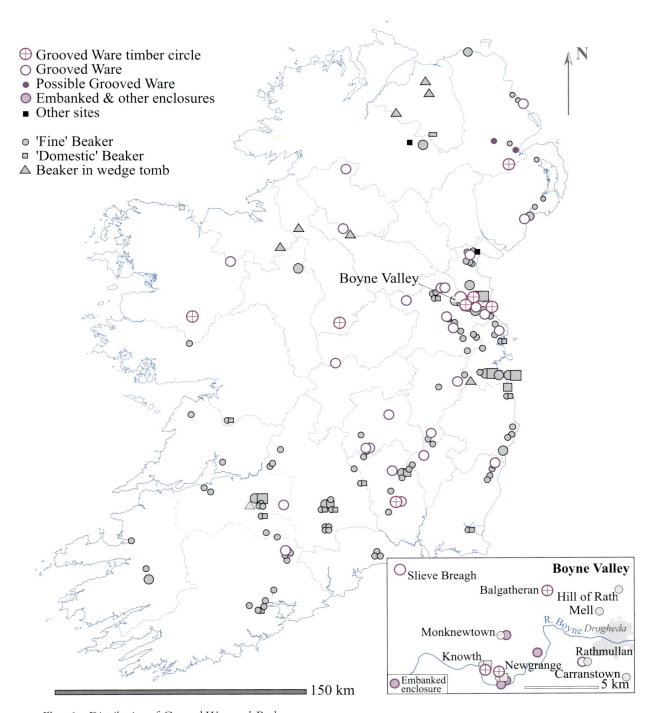

Illus. 6—Distribution of Grooved Ware and Beaker.

The Chalcolithic period (c. 2450–2300 BC)

With the introduction of copper metal-working came the widespread adoption of Beaker pottery. These vessels have generally simple rounded or pointed rims, S-shaped ('bell') profiles and flat bases. The fabric is fine and fired using techniques that differ from those of the preceding period and produce a typical 'sandwich' profile, with buff to red-buff or red-brown surfaces and grey to dark grey cores. These coil-built, thin-walled (≤ 5–7 mm) vessels frequently contain fine quartzite inclusions. A larger, thicker-walled variant, referred to as domestic, coarse or rusticated Beaker, occurs throughout the tradition (Illus. 7c). (These vessels, while generally larger and heavier, are not appreciably 'coarser' than the so-called 'fine' wares. Rustication refers specifically to decoration with fingernail, or sometimes bird bone, impressions frequently arranged haphazardly over the entire vessel.) Pots of this type may have been specialist storage or cooking vessels, but all Beaker in Ireland, whether 'fine' or 'coarse', is primarily domestic in function (Illus. 7c).

Decoration consists principally of horizontally arranged bands of incised, cord- or comb-impressed lines, with intervening blank zones or panels filled with oblique, chevron or lattice ornament (Illus. 7a). There is a very small number of vessels covered with horizontal lines ('All-Over Ornament'): these represent one of the earliest components of the tradition (Illus. 7b). Other decorative elements include pinched-up horizontal cordons: these occur on fine Beakers but are a particular feature of the domestic variant, as are stab-marks (fingernail or bone) and scored lines. There are a few other vessel shapes in the Irish repertoire: these include flat-bottomed bowls at Newgrange (Cleary 1983), footed ('polypod') bowls (possibly based on wooden prototypes: Earwood 1991/2) from Newgrange, Mell and Newtownbalregan, Co. Louth, and Blackglen, Co. Dublin (Illus. 7b) (Cleary 1983; McQuade 2005; Roycroft 2005, 74; Grogan & Roche 2005b; 2009a), and shallow dishes or lids at Kilgobbin and Paulstown (Hagen 2004; Elliot 2008; Grogan 2004b; Grogan & Roche 2009b). Plain vessels—with or, more frequently, without cordons—are also common (Illus. 7d). These forms and decorative styles have generally been assigned to Clarke's (1970) European Bell Beaker type or his North Rhine or Wessex/Middle Rhine types. Following reviews by, for example, Lanting & van der Waals (1972), there has been a greater recognition of the regional development of Beaker. Case's (1993) simpler threefold scheme, and its specific application to the Irish material, provides a straightforward medium for insular comparison (Case 1995). The formal horizontally zoned decoration on many of the Irish vessels belongs to his style 2 and is widely dated to 2450–2300 BC.

There are a few sites with late Beakers; these have more angular and often squatter profiles with more vertically arranged ornament. Both early and late Beakers occur at Dalkey Island, while later forms occur at Ballyedmonduff, Caherabbey Upper, Co. Tipperary, Raheenagurren West, Co. Wexford, and Knockadoon site C, Co. Limerick (Ó Ríordáin & de Valera 1952; McQuade et al. 2009; Breen 2007a; 2007b, 8–9; Ó Ríordáin 1954; Grogan & Roche 2009c; 2008b).

Illus. 7 (opposite page)—Beaker (Chalcolithic) pottery: (A–B, H–I) Windmill, Co. Tipperary; (C–D) Farranamanagh, Co. Tipperary; (G) Dalkey Island (after Liversage 1968); (E, J–L) Mell, Co. Louth; (F, M–R) Newtownbalregan 2, Co. Louth; (S) polypod bowl from Newtownbalregan; (T–U) Kilgobbin, Co. Dublin. Beaker distributions (inset): (a) horizontally zoned ornament with fringes; (b) horizontally zoned ornament; (c) 'fine' plain vessels; (d) 'Rockbarton'-type 'domestic' vessels.

Clay and fire: the development and distribution of pottery traditions in prehistoric Ireland

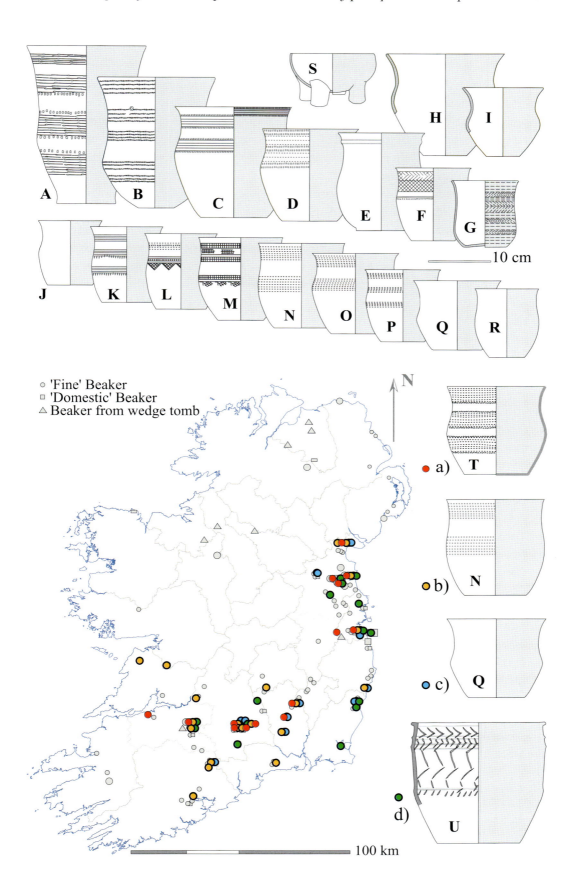

The vast majority of the Beaker-associated sites are domestic (over 120 Beaker sites have now been recorded). Typically, these are represented by pits, fireplaces, spreads or deposits of occupation debris and occasional post-holes; while many produced only small quantities (less than 50 sherds), several contained large assemblages, as at, for example, Mell, Knowth, Newgrange, Kilgobbin, Dalkey Island and several sites at Lough Gur (Illus. 6). House plans have only occasionally been identified, e.g. at Newgrange (Grogan 2004a, fig. 9.3) and Graigueshoneen, Co. Waterford (Tierney et al. 2008), but the evidence suggests that domestic dwellings were circular and required only light foundations that are difficult to identify archaeologically. Burial associations in wedge tombs, at Lough Gur, Moytirra, Co. Sligo, Ballyedmonduff, Co. Dublin, Aughrim, Co. Cavan, and Ballybriest, Co. Derry (Ó Ríordáin & Ó h-Iceadha 1955; Madden 1969; Ó Ríordáin & de Valera 1952; Hurl 1998; Channing 1993), suggest that these are the principal funerary focus in some parts of the country (O'Brien 1999). There are a few secondary burials in other tomb types, including 11 court tombs (Herity 1987) and Knowth (Eogan 1984), but no other definite burials. Sherds were found in association with copper-mining work at Ross Island, Co. Kerry (O'Brien 1995).

The Early Bronze Age (c. 2200–1600 BC)

There is a very considerable body of ceramic evidence from this period, consisting of at least 2,000 individual vessels (Illus. 8 & 9). Many of these have been recovered intact, or substantially complete, from burials. In contrast to the rest of the prehistoric evidence, the majority of the associations are funerary; the pottery comes from cists and pits in both isolated graves and cemeteries (Waddell 1990; Grogan 2004c; Mount 1995). This material has been very well served by a number of studies (Brindley 1980; Kavanagh 1973; 1976; 1977; Longworth 1984; Ó Ríordáin & Waddell 1993; Waddell 1995) and both the sequence and dating of the pottery types are well developed (Brindley 2007a). For this reason only a brief overview of the pottery is presented here.

There is a general sequence—bowls, Vase Tradition (vases, vase and encrusted urns), collared and cordoned urns—although there is considerable overlap between some of the individual types. Miniature 'accessory vessels' form an occasional aspect of the burial traditions (Kavanagh 1977). A wide range of decorative techniques and motifs are represented, particularly on bowls, vases and encrusted urns. Despite the clear classifications there is considerable variation within each group, emphasising the one-off context of production and the design contribution of individual potters. Nevertheless, a few regional groups have been identified, such as the biconical bowls concentrated in the Kildare area (Sheridan 1993, 57, fig. 25).

Compared to the large existing data set there are only a small number of recent discoveries. These include important cemeteries at Carn More 5, Co. Louth, Paulstown, Co.

Illus. 8 (opposite page)—Early Bronze Age bowls and vases. (A) Simple bowl: 'Mountfield', Co. Tyrone; (B) necked bipartite bowl: Crouck (Dun Ruadh), Co. Tyrone; (C) tripartite bowl: Rush, Co. Dublin; (D) tripartite bowl: Nurney Demesne, Co. Kildare; (E) ribbed bowls: Graney West, Co. Kildare; (F) tripartite vase: Topped Mountain (Mullyknock), Co. Fermanagh; (G) bipartite vase: Moylarg, Co. Antrim (all from Ó Ríordáin & Waddell 1993, figs 1, 4, 6, 8 and 10). (Distribution sources: Ó Ríordáin & Waddell 1993, with additions.)

Clay and fire: the development and distribution of pottery traditions in prehistoric Ireland

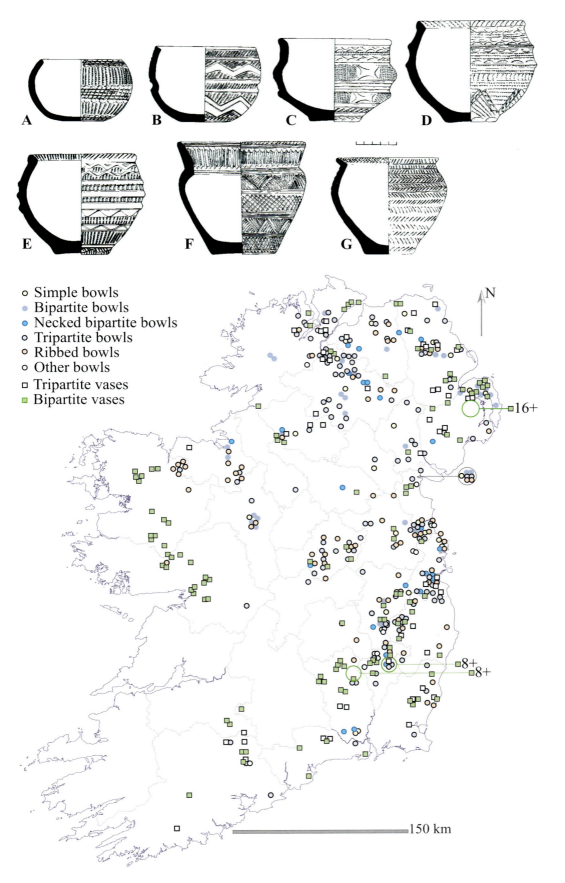

Creative Minds

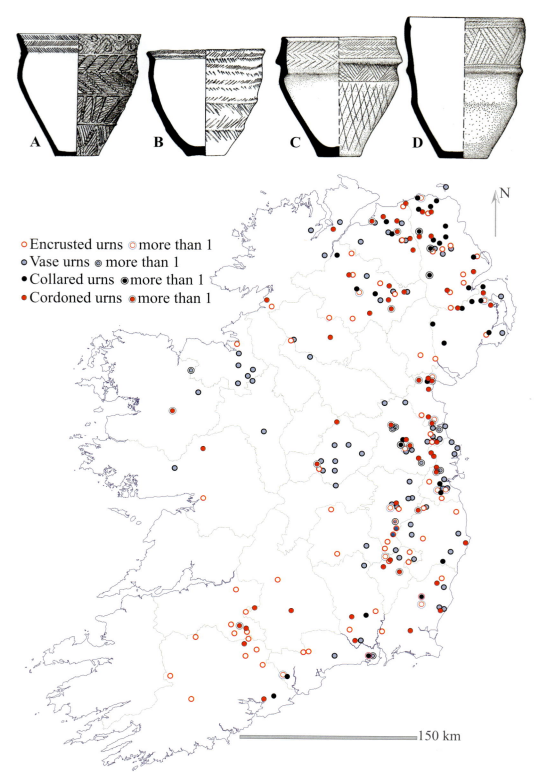

Illus. 9—Early Bronze Age cinerary urns. (A) Encrusted urn: Clonshannon, Co. Wicklow (Kavanagh 1973, fig. 36, no. 87); (B) vase urn: Cloghskelt, Co. Down (Brindley 2007a, fig. 158–III.23); (C) collared urn: 'County Down' (Kavanagh 1976, fig. 20.32); (D) cordoned urn: Knockadea, Co. Limerick (Kavanagh 1976, fig. 30.32). (Distribution sources: Kavanagh 1973; 1976; Brindley 2007a, with additions.)

Kilkenny, and a ritual enclosure, probably encompassing a disturbed cemetery, at Kilshane, Co. Dublin (Bayley 2006; Elliot 2008; Moore 2007; FitzGerald 2006, 33–5; Grogan & Roche 2006a; Roche & Grogan 2009b; 2005a). Most of the sites have emphasised the existing distribution patterns, with a particular emphasis on the eastern part of the country and large concentrations in some areas such as County Meath, the west Wicklow, Kildare and north Carlow region and the north-east.

The Middle Bronze Age (c. 1600–1100 BC)

By the end of the Early Bronze Age collared urns were no longer in use, although cordoned urns appear to have continued into the Middle Bronze Age. During this stage a domestic variant of the cordoned urn developed; this has less frequent and less orderly ornament, consisting of thick cord-impressed and, increasingly, scored lines (Illus. 10) (Grogan & Roche 2010; Waddell 1995, 113, 118; Brindley 2007a, 143; Kavanagh 1976, 330). Important assemblages include Ballybrowney Lower, Co. Cork (Cotter 2005; Roche & Grogan 2005b), and Knockhouse Lower, Co. Waterford (Richardson & Johnson 2007; Brindley 2007b). By around 1500 BC a plain domestic form of bucket- or barrel-shaped vessel emerged from this background. Both funerary and domestic associations occur, and sites include Corrstown, Co. Derry (Roche & Grogan 2008), and several in east Limerick, including Raheen, Shanaclogh and Mitchelstowndown North (Gowen 1988, 84–94, 68–72, 98–103). Burials can contain either upright or inverted vessels. Another emerging feature of this period is the deposition of broken pottery sherds, instead of complete pots, in simple cremation pits, as at Mitchelstowndown North, Co. Limerick, Killoran, Co. Tipperary, and Mounthawk, Co. Kerry (Gowen 1988; Stevens 2005; Dunne 1998). Unaccompanied cremations, in cists or more frequently in pits, which are an important component of the entire Bronze Age, become an even more common feature of the Middle to Late periods; during these stages the quantity of bone extracted from the pyre for burial is greatly reduced and represents only part of the human remains (Grogan et al. 2007). (Too few unaccompanied cremations have been accurately dated and this has created a serious deficit in our understanding of the chronological range of this aspect of prehistoric burial traditions.)

The Late Bronze Age (c. 1100–800 BC)

Plain, bucket-shaped domestic vessels continue to dominate: the pottery is slightly coarser and thicker, but generally better fired, than in the preceding period. There are a limited number of forms, although simple rounded, internally bevelled and occasionally broad, expanded rims suggest, with the wide range of sizes, a variety of functions (Illus. 10). Decoration is rare but includes thumbnail impressions or slashed lines on the rim top at, for example, Rathgall, Co. Wicklow, and Freestone Hill, Co. Kilkenny (Roche, forthcoming; Raftery 1969). Small perforations set in a row beneath the rim, designed to ventilate lidded vessels during storage or cooking, are an occasional feature at, for example, Rathgall and Navan Fort, Co. Armagh (Roche, forthcoming; McCorry 1997). The most common associations of Late Bronze Age plain wares are domestic, including hillforts at Rathgall, Haughey's Fort, Co. Armagh, Dún Aonghasa, Aran More, Co. Galway, and

Creative Minds

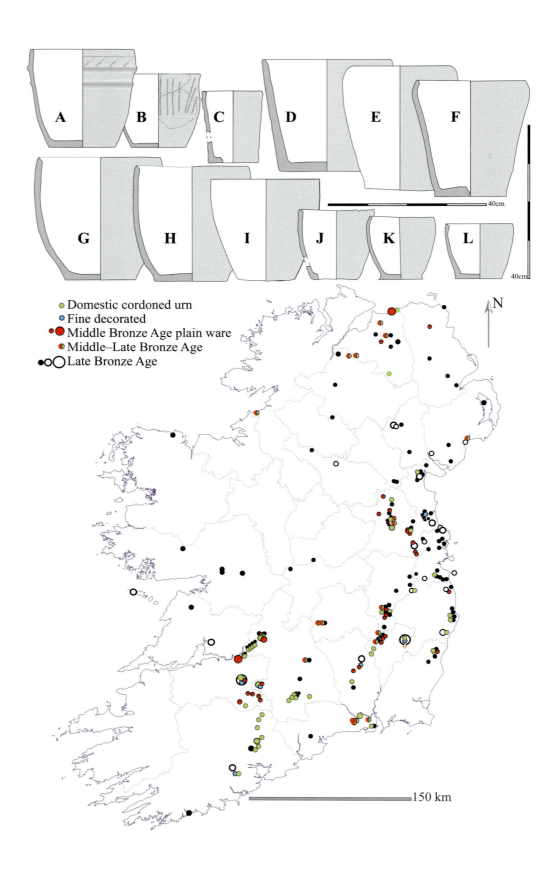

Mooghaun, Co. Clare (Raftery 1976; 1995; Roche, forthcoming; Mallory 1995; Cotter 1993; Grogan 2005). Other important assemblages include several sites at Lough Gur (Ó Ríordáin 1954; Grogan & Eogan 1987; Cleary 1995) and an enclosed settlement at Chancellorsland, Co. Tipperary (Doody 2008; Cleary 2008). This pottery also comes from funerary contexts, as at Kilbane, Co. Limerick, Priestsnewtown, Co. Wicklow, and Darcystown, Co. Dublin, where the pots act as upright or inverted containers for cremations in pits (O'Callaghan 2006; Tobin et al. 2004; Carroll et al. 2008; Grogan & Roche 2004a; 2004b; 2008c; 2008d). Ceremonial sites include Lugg, Co. Dublin, and the Grange Stone Circle, Lough Gur (Kilbride-Jones 1950; Ó Ríordáin 1951; Roche & Eogan 2007; Roche 2004). Many of the vessels from ritual contexts show evidence, in the form of sooting or blackened accretions, for previous use in domestic contexts.

Middle to Late Bronze Age distribution patterns
Plain ware of the Middle Bronze Age has only been widely recognised recently and there remain difficulties in distinguishing this material, particularly in older discoveries: for that reason the distribution of this pottery is treated with that of the Late Bronze Age (Illus. 10). Recent infrastructural and peri-urban development has had the greatest impact on our knowledge of the distribution patterning of this period; nevertheless, despite the considerable number of new discoveries, it should be stressed that many sites of this period produce no ceramic evidence and are identified through radiocarbon dating or lithic associations. There are particular concentrations in north Leinster, and in this region these reflect continuity with earlier focal points. This includes the upland fringe on the northern slopes of the Dublin–Wicklow Mountains, the lowlands of Kildare, Carlow and north Kilkenny (broadly the Barrow Valley), and the lowland coastal zone of north Dublin and east Meath. There are also notably sparse areas, such as the central and north midlands, although even here there are important sites, such as Ballinderry 2 (Ballynahinch) and Tober, Co. Offaly (Hencken 1942; Walsh 2007; 2009; Grogan & Roche 2008e).

The Iron Age (c. 800 BC–AD 450)

Pottery continued to be made in Ireland until the end of the Bronze Age and possibly into the first, Hallstatt C, part of the Iron Age (800–700 BC). After this it appears that the manufacture of pottery ceased and was replaced, in terms of native production, by lathe-turned and stave-built wooden vessels and leather containers (see Raftery 1995). While there is no clear explanation for this cessation, there are no definite instances of local production in the Iron Age, although small quantities of pottery were imported from the Roman world in the early centuries AD.

Illus. 10 (opposite page)— Domestic cordoned urns: (A) Lough Gur, Site C, 1949 (Ó Ríordáin 1954, pl. 35.1); (B) Ballybrowney Lower, Co. Cork. Middle Bronze Age plain ware: (C) Raheen, Co. Limerick (Gowen 1988, fig. 43); (D) Athgarret, Co. Kildare (Sleeman & Cleary 1987, fig. 4.2); (E) Knockaholet, Co. Antrim (Henry 1934, pl. 28.2); (F) Circle P, Lough Gur (Grogan & Eogan 1987, pl. 23). Late Bronze Age domestic: (G) Haughey's Fort, Co. Armagh (Mallory 1988, fig. 7); (H) Lough Gur, Circle L (Grogan & Eogan 1987, fig. 51.V.35); (I) Haughey's Fort (Mallory 1988, fig. 7); (J) Lough Gur, Circle L (Grogan & Eogan 1987, fig. 51); (K) Lough Eskragh, Co. Tyrone (Waddell 1998, fig. 124); (L) Carrig, Co. Wicklow.

Conclusion

It is clear that pottery was one of the most common elements of prehistoric equipment, used for storage, cooking and ritual activity, including accompanying the dead into the afterlife. During most of the period the same types of pottery, and even occasionally the same pots, were used in each of these roles. The changing fashion for different shapes and decorative treatments reflects wider contacts, particularly with Britain, that highlight the network of communication and interaction that nurtured Irish prehistoric communities.

While there is an absence of identifiable kilns (prehistoric pottery was produced in so-called bonfire kilns, which are simple pits with a temporary covering) or production sites (characterised by waste material and the remnants of unsuccessful firings), it is apparent that most, if not virtually all, pottery was locally manufactured. It appears that production took place at the basic level of the 'family' or community, with the task probably assigned to the most adept member of each group. During the Early Bronze Age it is possible that there was some more specialist output catering for the increased demand for high-quality funerary vessels. At other times, however, and particularly during the Middle to Late Bronze Age, pottery was essentially utilitarian, requiring minimal levels of skill. Another basic feature of the Irish evidence that indicates the essentially functional role of most pottery is the very rare incidence of repaired pots. An interesting exception is provided by two collared urns from Monamintra, Co. Waterford, that appear to have been hastily repaired immediately before placement in Early Bronze Age graves (Lalonde 2008; Grogan & Roche 2009d; 2010b).

Given the attraction of modelling clay (and pastry dough!) for modern children, it is perhaps surprising that we have no examples of simple playthings, although some small hemispherical cups from Lough Gur could represent the product of little fingers. Interestingly, we do not have any obvious 'practice pieces' either; possibly there were some long-standing taboos or restrictions associated with pottery production. In this regard, another absence in the record is that of representational art or decoration; with the exception of the extraordinary, and unique, Early Bronze Age 'face-mask' pot from Mitchelstown, Co. Cork (Kiely & Sutton 2007; Grogan & Roche 2006b), there are no examples of human or animal images, either as shapes or as two-dimensional renditions.

As noted at the beginning of this paper, a significant number of new data, and very large amounts of prehistoric pottery, have come into the record in the past ten years, especially as a result of the large number of excavations undertaken in advance of construction of the new road network. Much of this has confirmed known patterns, in terms of spatial distribution and human activity, but is providing new insights particularly in terms of how the material culture was used and deployed by prehistoric societies. The new material has also greatly extended our knowledge of the range and density of human settlement for many periods. In three areas, for example, the south Leinster and mid-Munster regions, and the western fringes from Kerry to Donegal, there has been a dramatic increase in sites identified during the past decade. Pottery, as one major component of the material assemblage, is both a conservative and occasionally sensitive indicator of social, ritual and economic development, and the new data have revealed many fruitful avenues of research into the lives of our prehistoric antecedents.

Acknowledgements

Much of this paper is based on analyses carried out for a variety of archaeological companies and institutions; we would particularly like to thank Archaeological Consultancy Services Ltd, Irish Archaeological Services Ltd, Margaret Gowen & Co. Ltd, Headland Archaeology (Ireland) Ltd, Valerie J Keeley Ltd, Thames Valley Archaeological Services (Ireland) Ltd, Arch-Tech Ltd, Eachtra Archaeological Projects, Aegis Archaeology Ltd, Judith Carroll and Co. Ltd, The Archaeology Company, Dan Noonan Associates, the National Museum of Ireland, the Ulster Museum, Queen's University, Belfast, the School of Archaeology, UCD, the Department of the Environment, Heritage and Local Government, and the National Roads Authority. Many colleagues have provided insight into aspects of the material and for this we are particularly grateful to Neil Carlin, Alison Sheridan, Fintan Walsh and George Eogan.

4. Ancient woodland use in the midlands: understanding environmental and landscape change through archaeological and palaeoecological techniques

Ellen OCarroll

The use and exploitation of trees, woods and forests have played a very important role in the history of humankind and the environment. Such use also provides some insight into and understanding of the creative minds of our ancestors. Unlike implements of pottery, metal and stone, however, wooden artefacts rarely survive long enough for us to study and classify as a means of understanding our past cultural heritage.

What survive most often at archaeological sites are the remains of charcoal and pollen from waterlogged deposits near to or at the excavated site. Charcoal can be present in features such as post-holes or slot-trenches, indicating the types of wood used as building material. Wood and its by-product charcoal were used as fuel for everyday use at domestic hearths and in association with metal-working activities. Recent excavations along many road schemes in Ireland have uncovered hundreds of charcoal production pits where oak wood was converted into charcoal for metal-working and industrial uses from prehistory until recent times (see Kenny, Chapter 8). Specific wood types such as oak were selected and used in cremation burial rites (O'Donnell 2007). Wood was also a key raw material in the manufacture of tools and containers (O'Sullivan 1990).

Pollen analysis, the study of vegetation history by counting the microfossils of pollen grains, is a technique used for reconstructing woodland succession as well as the scale and type of vegetation that was present in close proximity to archaeological remains. Pollen analysis can also reveal the impact of both humans and climate on that vegetation in the past.

By combining the analysis of wood selection and use, which is intrinsically linked to human influence, with a record of pollen data from sediment cores it is possible to recreate past landscapes. Linking palaeoenvironmental and archaeological research has become an increasingly important method of understanding past landscape and societal change in Ireland, and an NRA-funded Ph.D research project is currently adopting this approach in assessing ancient landscape change in the midlands (see below).

Wood and charcoal analysis

Each wood taxon (one or more organisms classified as a group) has a distinct microstructure, and charcoal and wood can therefore be identified to species level under a high-powered microscope. When slivers of wood or charcoal are examined in this way, the patterns in their microstructure are compared to known species or reference keys and the identifications are made (Illus. 1).

Pollen analysis

Pollen grains are dispersed into the air by vegetation and can accumulate in sediments in lakes, peat bogs and waterlogged ditches, building up sequentially. Sediments are extracted

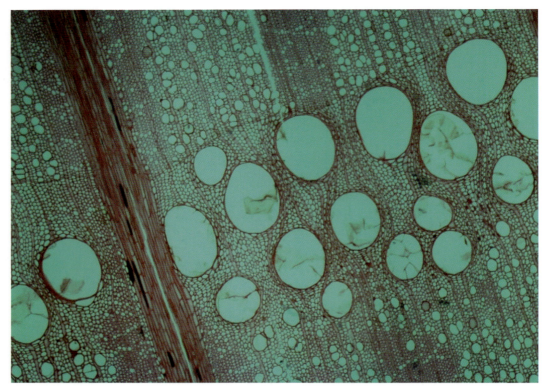

Illus. 1—Microstructure of oak (Quercus sp.): a transverse section showing wide ray and tree-ring growth (Lorna O'Donnell).

Illus. 2—Extracting a pollen core from Ballinderry Lough, Co. Westmeath (Ellen OCarroll).

for study by coring to obtain a vertical sequence of sediments deposited at particular times (Illus. 2). Samples are then taken from the core at 1 cm intervals and examined under a high-powered microscope. As the outer surface of a pollen grain is highly durable, pollen is preserved in sediments and is available for identification and counting. Each grain is different in structure and shape; by identifying the quantity and variety of pollen grains at each level in the past, one can reconstruct the types of vegetation that existed in any given area (Moore et al. 1991). This analysis results in the creation of a pollen diagram, which is a graphical expression of the frequency of the different types of pollen over time, with radiocarbon dating of organic samples from the core providing a chronological framework.

Baronstown 1—a case-study from the M3

An example of linking palaeoenvironmental and archaeological research is provided by the investigation of a 'defensive or military' ringfort at Baronstown, Co. Meath, which was excavated by Stephen Linnane of Archaeological Consultancy Services Ltd in advance of the construction of the M3 Clonee to North of Kells motorway scheme (Linnane & Kinsella 2007; 2009a; 2009b).[1] The impressive ringfort ditch was 4 m wide and 3 m deep and was surrounded by numerous smaller enclosing features, two possible houses and cereal-drying kilns (Illus. 3).

A total of 492 wood fragments (artefacts, stakes, chips etc.) from Baronstown were analysed by the author for species identification, wood use and woodworking (Illus. 4). The artefact assemblage included numerous yew cask and bucket staves and stave fragments (Illus. 5), a lathe-turned alder bowl, an alder scoop/ladle (Illus. 6), two possible pegs/dowels (of ash and hazel), an ash rod, a dowelled yew object, a hazel withy (rope) and a possible handle/tenon of blackthorn. The samples were identified as alder (*Alnus glutinosa*; 28

Illus. 3—Aerial view of the impressive 'military' ringfort at Baronstown, Co. Meath (Studio Lab).

Creative Minds

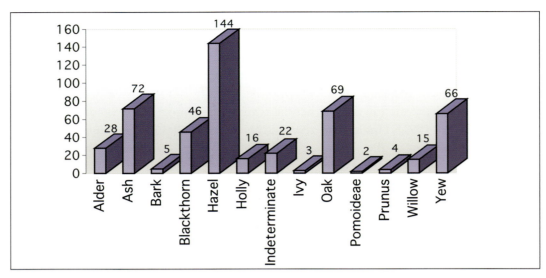

Illus. 4—Wood species identifications from Baronstown (Ellen OCarroll).

Illus. 5—Yew cask stave from Baronstown (John Sunderland).

Illus. 6—Carved alder scoop from Baronstown (John Sunderland).

samples), ash (*Fraxinus excelsior*; 72 samples), blackthorn (*Prunus spinosa*; 46 samples), hazel (*Corylus avellana*; 144 samples), holly (*Ilex aquifolium*; 16 samples), ivy (*Hedera helix*; three samples), Pomoideae (hawthorn, mountain ash, apple and pear; two samples), blackthorn/cherry (*Prunus* sp.; four samples), oak (*Quercus* sp.; 69 samples), willow (*Salix* sp.; 15 samples) and yew (*Taxus baccata*; 66 samples).

The wood selected for making the tools and containers demonstrates that the inhabitants of the site had an in-depth understanding and knowledge of the attributes of the various wood species. For instance, yew would have been selected for the manufacture of the staves because it is strong, very elastic and durable, and objects made from it rarely warp or crack. It is clear from the wood analysis that the wood from Baronstown could not all have been derived from the same source. A variety of woodlands were exploited: broad-leaved, wet, coppiced and scrub woodlands.

When a wider landscape approach is taken through the analysis of pollen from the basal fills of the Baronstown ditches we get a somewhat different picture. The pollen identified was principally from herbaceous taxa, including some cereals, with a few arboreal (tree) taxa represented, including alder, birch, hazel and oak (Archaeological Services Durham University 2009). The lower levels of tree pollen relative to herbaceous pollen are to be expected, as pollen studies from other sites throughout Ireland suggest that large-scale destruction of the major woodlands had taken place during the later Iron Age to provide land for farming (Mitchell 1987, 121). The results of the pollen analysis do not indicate any high numbers of yew trees in the area, which is significant given the quantity of yew staves/stave fragments recovered from the site. Another absent tree pollen is ash, which is surprising as ash was the second most dominant taxon identified from the wood assemblage. The different pictures may be related to a number of factors, such as different periods for the dispersal of the pollen in the ditches and the use of the wood on site, variable decomposition rates of specific pollen types in certain soils, as well as the possibility of trade in yew for the manufacture of wooden staves. The pollen may in this particular case be a reflection of the very local landscape close to the ditches, while the wood analysis is perhaps a more accurate reflection of the woods present in the vicinity and surrounding environment of the site, as well as of the wood selected for use at the site.

Analysis of the findings from Baronstown highlights the importance of a multidisciplinary approach to include a tightly dated pollen core that links in with the actual archaeological on-site activity. If the wooden artefacts had not survived and pollen was the only indicator, it is clear that the importance of yew and ash to the people who occupied the site would not have been readily recognised.

NRA Research Fellowship Programme

In 2008 the NRA awarded funding from its Research Fellowship Programme to the author to conduct a Ph.D research project entitled *Understanding environmental and landscape change in the midlands of Ireland through the cultural use of woodland*. This research is being undertaken at the Botany Department, Trinity College, Dublin, and is combining palaeoecological techniques and archaeological data (including information derived from NRA-funded excavations) in order to quantify woodland use and its impact in the Irish midlands since the Mesolithic period (c. 8000–4000 BC).

This research project has two principal aims. The first is to create a detailed and consolidated reconstruction of the woodland environment and its use from the Mesolithic period to the present day along two new sections of the N6 route in counties Westmeath and Offaly (initially the N6 Kilbeggan–Athlone Dual Carriageway was the main focus of the project, but now archaeological investigations on the N6 Kinnegad–Kilbeggan Dual Carriageway will also be addressed). Considerable resources have been invested in archaeological site investigations in this region over the past five years, and the detailed analysis of woodland exploitation will offer an ideal framework within which to link past human exploitation of the area with the surrounding environment. Furthermore, these sections of the N6 boast unrivalled data sources, from the quantity of NRA-funded excavations undertaken in the area, to enable the completion of a thoroughly comprehensive investigation. This aim will be achieved by marrying environmental archaeological and palaeoecological techniques. The second aim is to develop a series of recommendations and guidelines for the sampling and analysis of wood, charcoal and pollen on or near archaeological remains for use by field archaeologists working on future NRA-funded archaeological investigations.

Although this study is at a preliminary stage, some interesting results and trends are emerging; these are outlined below.

N6 study area

The route of the new 57-km-long N6 Kilbeggan–Athlone Dual Carriageway in counties Offaly and Westmeath was the main focus of the multidisciplinary environmental research at the outset (Illus. 7). Archaeological investigation along the Kilbeggan–Athlone section identified over 86 archaeological sites reflecting approximately 6,000 years of human activity in the area. The range of sites excavated along the road scheme and included in the study includes some small-scale Neolithic activity, two Bronze Age settlement sites and numerous burnt mounds (*fulachta fiadh*), Iron Age metal-working sites and industrial activity (e.g. cereal-drying kilns and charcoal production pits), and an early medieval ringfort. Two significant complexes in County Offaly were also excavated, comprising a Late Bronze Age settlement/ritual site at Tober (Walsh 2007) and a multiphase enclosure at Cappydonnell Big (Coughlan 2007; 2009b).

Although some substantial medieval sites were excavated along the N6, the bulk of the remains were prehistoric, mostly Bronze Age in date and associated with burnt mound activity. This is in contrast to the previously documented archaeological sites in the study area recorded in the Record of Monuments and Places (RMP), which are more indicative of a fossil medieval landscape comprising ecclesiastical and secular sites.

Driving from Kinnegad to Athlone along the new M6 motorway today, one would be mistaken in thinking that this was always a landscape largely devoid of trees. Throughout various periods over the last 5,000 years the area would have been densely wooded, and the surrounding woodlands would have been integral to the life and, indeed, survival of our ancestors. The wood and charcoal identified from the excavated sites would have been selected for specific purposes, and therefore it is important to compare the wood analysis with the pollen record. This provides a full and accurate picture of the surrounding landscape and the changes wrought by human influences and interactions. This area of work

Ancient woodland use in the midlands

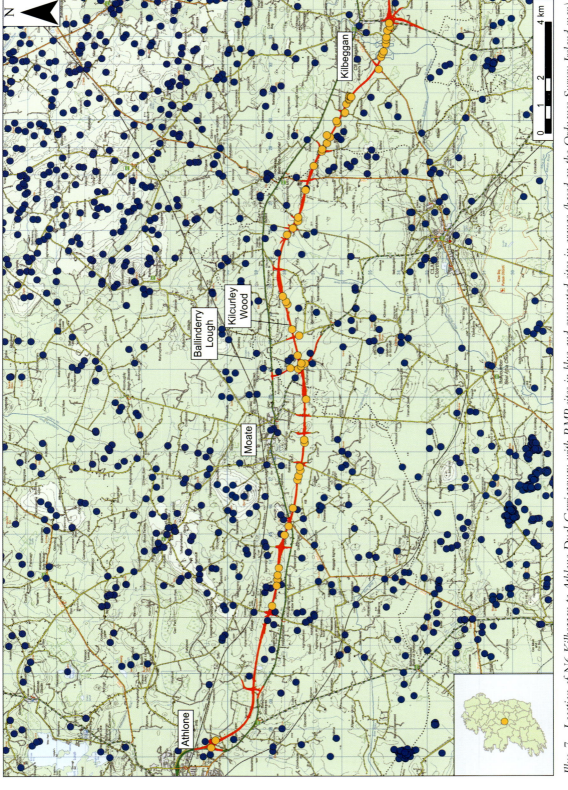

Illus. 7—Location of N6 Kilbeggan to Athlone Dual Carriageway, with RMP sites in blue and excavated sites in orange (based on the Ordnance Survey Ireland map).

is especially important in Ireland, where there are very few written records up to the 18th century relating to the quantity and type of woodland in Ireland (McCracken 1971). These complementary approaches form the basis of palaeoecological reconstruction and archaeological modelling of woodland exploitation and use in Ireland.

Pollen work

To help interpret changes in the wider landscape, thereby linking the environment to the archaeological data sets from the N6, a regional pollen core and a local pollen core have been extracted from two locations within the study area. A long pollen core extracted from Ballinderry Lough, Co. Westmeath, 2 km east of Moate, will provide a tightly dated sequence of vegetation change in the surrounding area, focusing on a 30-km radius (Illus. 2 & 7). This is in contrast to a shorter pollen core extracted from a closed-canopy woodland in Kilcurley Wood, Co. Westmeath, 2 km south-east of Ballinderry Lough, where a more localised and shorter vegetation history will be studied (Illus. 7). These two cores will facilitate a comparative evaluation of the local vegetation (woodland) and a more regional record of vegetation change (lake) throughout the Holocene period (9500 BC to present) in the midlands.

Preliminary analysis of the regional pollen core from Ballinderry Lough is ongoing at the time of writing. Further radiocarbon dates and analysis at a tighter resolution along the core are required to highlight specific changes in the landscape at particular periods and to identify human activity in the study area. The provisional results show a noticeable decline in woodland cover as the Holocene progresses. For instance, during the Bronze Age (c. 2400–800 BC), which is characterised by a rise in archaeological monuments and, by inference, population in the area, there is an opening up of the landscape. This is evidenced in the core by a rise in ribwort (*Plantago lanceolata*), a common weed of cultivated land, and a corresponding drop in oak (*Quercus*) and ash (*Fraxinus excelsior*) trees. The decline of woodland would have continued apace as human settlement expanded across the region in subsequent periods. By AD 1700 there is a conspicuous drop in hazel (*Corylus avellana*), oak, alder (*Alnus glutinosa*) and elm (*Ulmus* sp.) pollen towards the top of the core, which most likely relates to clearance of the woodland landscape during the Plantation period. This decrease in woodland pollen is noted in other cores from the midlands, such as that from Monaincha, Co. Tipperary (Hall 2003). There is also a corresponding rise in pine pollen during this post-1700 period.

Overall, the pollen diagram indicates the development of bog and marshland throughout the study area, with plenty of heather (*Calluna*) and sedges (Cyperaceae) recorded from along the latter half of the core, as well as scrub woodland and pastoral grasslands.

Previous pollen cores extracted and analysed from Cornaher Lough, Co. Meath (Heery 1998), at the eastern side of the N6 study area, and Clara Bog, Co. Offaly (Connolly 1999), to the south of the current N6, will also be studied to examine vegetation change in relation to human activity in the study area.

Charcoal and wood analysis

The research is more advanced in relation to the identification of charcoal and wood from the excavated sites on the N6 Kilbeggan–Athlone Dual Carriageway. A total of 17 wood taxa have been identified from charcoal samples from 55 of the 86 sites. The range of sites analysed includes small-scale Neolithic activity (pits and one possible structure), 27 Bronze

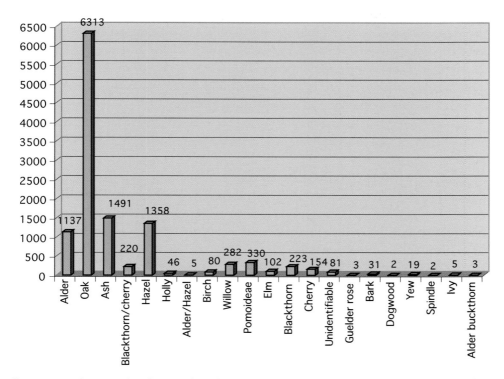

Illus. 8—Wood species identifications from charcoal recovered during excavations along the N6 (Ellen O'Carroll).

Age burnt mounds, two Late Bronze Age habitation sites, one Iron Age metal-working site, two early medieval ringforts and six sites consisting of cereal-drying kilns and charcoal production pits, a multiperiod enclosure and 10 miscellaneous hearths and pits (mostly dating from the medieval period). Wood samples from the troughs of various burnt mounds were also analysed (see below).

The 17 taxa identified from the charcoal samples (Illus. 8), in order of representation, were oak (*Quercus* sp.; 6,313 fragments), ash (*Fraxinus excelsior*; 1,491 fragments), hazel (*Corylus avellana*; 1,358 fragments), alder (*Alnus glutinosa*; 1,137 fragments), Pomoideae (hawthorn, mountain ash, apple, pear; 330 fragments), willow (*Salix* sp.; 282 fragments), blackthorn/cherry (*Prunus* sp.; 220 fragments), blackthorn (*Prunus spinosa*; 223 fragments), cherry (*Prunus avium/padus*; 154 fragments), elm (*Ulmus* sp.; 102 fragments), birch (*Betula* sp.; 80 fragments), holly *(Ilex aquifolium*; 46 fragments), yew (*Taxus baccata*; 19 fragments), ivy (*Hedera helix*; five fragments), alder buckthorn (*Frangula alnus*; three fragments), guelder rose (*Viburnum opulus*; three fragments), spindle (*Euonymus europaeus*; two fragments) and dogwood (*Cornus sanguina*; two fragments). A total of 81 fragments were unidentifiable and 19 fragments were identified as bark.

Analysis of the results indicates that samples from the Neolithic sites consisted almost exclusively of oak. The lack of Neolithic habitation evidence within the study area, coupled with the charcoal identification, suggests that a largely wooded landscape was present throughout much of the midlands 5,000 years ago and this may have inhibited wide-scale settlement. This hypothesis will be tested by the data collected from the pollen cores along the N6.

Oak also played a major role in the Early Bronze Age, but by the later Bronze Age hazel and ash were more common, which may indicate a more open landscape cleared by people who came to occupy the area during the period. Elm charcoal was also identified in greater quantities from the Early Bronze Age samples. Oak was selected for structural purposes at the Late Bronze Age habitation site at Tober. It was also dominant in the Iron Age and its use was presumably related to increased iron-working activities. Oak was almost exclusively collected for use in charcoal production pits during the early to later medieval period. Alder appears not to have played as significant a role, particularly during the Bronze Age with regard to burnt mounds.

Eighty-two wood samples were analysed from the trough linings associated with some of the burnt mounds. Oak was generally selected for use as planks, particularly in the Early Bronze Age, although alder planks were used to line one trough of Middle Bronze Age date. A variety of wood types were used as posts and stakes, although ash and hazel were more often selected for such constructional uses.

Conclusion

Woodland resources were integral to everyday life in the past. Our ancient ancestors had an in-depth knowledge of woodlands: wood use analysis clearly demonstrates that their selection of wood for utensils, structures and fuel was based on a firm understanding of the characteristics of the different species.

Further work using the complementary approaches of pollen, charcoal and wood analysis in association with the results of archaeological excavation along the N6 will provide a detailed reconstruction of woodland environment and usage through various periods in the midlands of counties Offaly and Westmeath.

Acknowledgements

I would like to thank my Ph.D supervisor, Professor Fraser Mitchell, for his helpful comments on this paper and for his supervision and guidance throughout the project. Thanks also to Fintan Walsh and all at Irish Archaeological Consultancy Ltd, who were most helpful in the gathering of samples and plans, and to the staff at Archaeological Consultancy Services Ltd, who kindly provided background information on Baronstown 1. Lastly, I would like to thank the NRA for funding and for providing necessary data and maps in the preparation of this paper, in particular Rónán Swan, Head of Archaeology (acting), and Orlaith Egan, NRA Archaeologist.

Note

1. NGR 294401, 259365; height 107 m OD; excavation reg. no. E3070; ministerial direction no. A008; excavation director Steve Linnane.

5. Reinventing the wheel: new evidence from Edercloon, Co. Longford

Caitríona Moore and Chiara Chiriotti

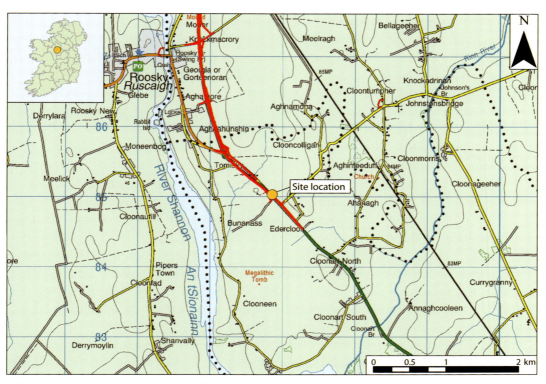

Illus. 1—Location of site at Edercloon, Co. Longford (based on the Ordnance Survey Ireland map).

The invention of the wheel is often lauded as one of the greatest of human achievements and is believed to have occurred independently at least twice: in Eurasia around the fourth millennium BC and in Mesoamerica at c. 200 BC–AD 200 (Mallory 2004, 134). Recently archaeologists working at Edercloon, Co. Longford, on the route of the N4 Dromod–Roosky Bypass uncovered exciting new evidence for the use and manufacture of wheels in prehistoric and early Ireland.

Edercloon is in the north-west corner of County Longford, just south of the County Leitrim border and the village of Roosky in County Roscommon (Illus. 1). The archaeological site at Edercloon was first identified in February 2006 during test excavations in a small tract of reclaimed raised bog, adjacent to the former N4. Subsequent excavations, carried out from April to September, uncovered what is now understood to be one of the most remarkable wetland archaeological complexes ever to be investigated in Ireland.[1] The test-trenching and full excavation were conducted by CRDS Ltd on behalf of Leitrim County Council, Longford County Council and the NRA.

The Edercloon complex

The archaeological site at Edercloon contained 45 individual structures, all built of wood, which, despite reclamation and drainage in the early part of the last century, were perfectly preserved by the wet, anaerobic (oxygen-free) qualities of the bog. These structures ranged from very large multiphase toghers (from the Irish *tóchar*) or trackways to short footpaths, small platforms and simple deposits of worked wood (Moore 2008, 2–6). The structures dated from the Neolithic to the early medieval period, and clearly this part of Edercloon bog was an important focal point within the surrounding landscape. This was particularly the case in the centuries of the Late Bronze Age (c. 1000–700 BC) to Early Iron Age (c. 700–200 BC), during which a network of very large trackways and associated platforms was built (Illus. 2).

Dense concentrations of sites have been identified previously in Ireland's raised bogs (e.g. Raftery 1996; McDermott et al. 2002; Murray et al. 2002; Gowen & Ó Néill 2005, 1), but the profusion of very large sites within a relatively small area, as at Edercloon, is unparalleled. While this alone is unusual, the Edercloon complex has several more atypical features, including interconnecting trackways with meandering routes, several structures of immense scale and depth, and repeated deposition of artefacts within structures. The Edercloon artefact assemblage is one of the largest collections of wooden objects ever to be archaeologically recovered from a raised bog in Ireland, and is believed to represent a distinct Late Bronze Age/Early Iron Age practice of votive deposition at the site (Moore, forthcoming). It includes bowls, spears, tool handles and many items of undetermined function. The remains of three wooden wheels, of varying form and date, were included within the assemblage and represent the first instance in Ireland where archaeologists have discovered wheels and trackways in direct association.

None of the three wheels from Edercloon have been directly dated, largely owing to issues of conservation, but material from the layers of the trackways from which they were recovered has been dated by radiocarbon dating and dendrochronology (tree-ring dating). In the case of two of the finds, the EDC 5 block wheel and the EDC 12/13 wheel rim, material physically associated with and believed to have been deposited at the same time as the objects has been dated. The dating of the third find, from the trackway EDC 49, is problematic: although the trackway itself has been dated, the date of the wheel remains in question (see below).

Ireland's earliest wheel

A portion of a block wheel is not only the earliest wheel fragment from Edercloon but is also the earliest evidence for the wheel in Ireland. It was found buried within the base of the large trackway EDC 5 (Illus. 3), and a piece of birch brushwood that directly overlay it has been radiocarbon-dated to 1206–970 BC (Wk-20961; see Appendix 1 for details). Additional dendrochronological dating of an oak roundwood from the same layer but from a different area of the trackway returned a date of 1120 BC ± 9 years or later (Q11026). This find represents approximately one third of a complete wheel and consists of a slightly asymmetrical C-shaped piece of alder measuring 1,190 mm long, 380 mm wide and 70 mm thick. The outer edge has been carved into a rounded C-shape, although the curve is incomplete in the centre and is cut straight for a length of 405 mm (Illus. 4). This straight

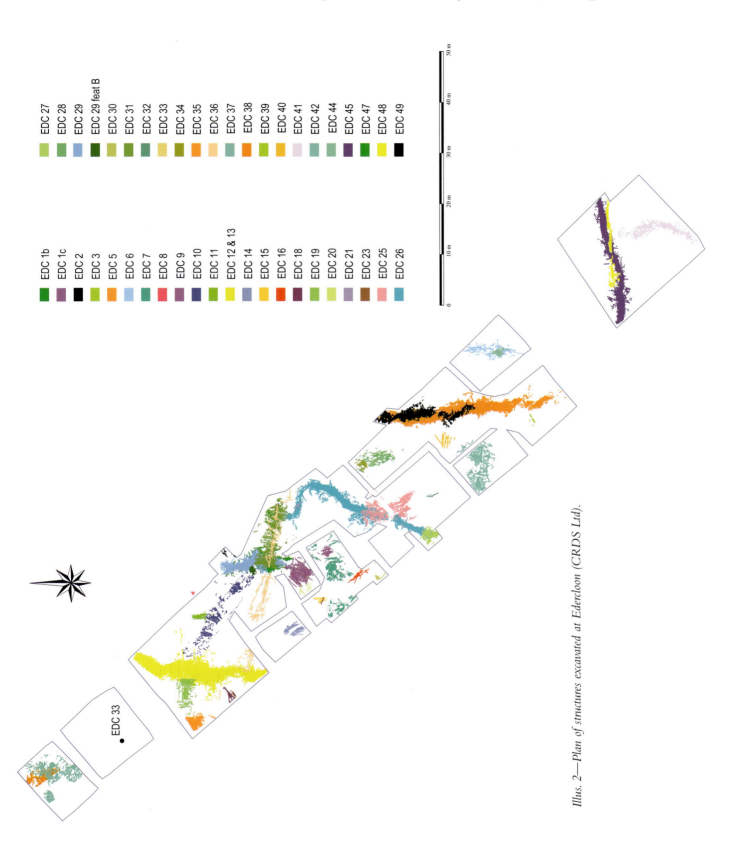

Illus. 2—Plan of structures excavated at Edercloon (CRDS Ltd).

Illus. 3—Edercloon block wheel fragment in situ (CRDS Ltd).

section is very close to what would have been the outer part of the tree, probably just beneath the bark. The inner edge of the wheel is also carved into a C-shape, known as a lunate opening (Lucas 1972, 22). At its outermost tips the corners have been trimmed off at an angle. There are two very distinct sides to the Edercloon block wheel. That which was deposited facing upwards is finely worked and is covered with almost 140 clean, crisp marks of a sharp-bladed tool, probably an adze. The opposite side, which lay on the bog surface, is worked to a much lesser extent and for the most part appears to be a simple cleft surface, with little additional finishing.

There is no doubt that this artefact is part of a tripartite block wheel, an early form of wheel previously dated in Ireland to the Iron Age (ibid., 19). Tripartite wheels were made with two pieces similar to the Edercloon find, between which was placed a third piece rounded at each end with a central circular opening through which the axle was placed. The three separate pieces were then secured together with large transverse dowels (ibid., 21). Bronze Age and Iron Age examples of this type of wheel have been found in Germany, Denmark and the Netherlands (Piggott 1983, 107–8, 197–8; van der Waals 1964, 121–6). Only a small number of block wheels have been found in Ireland but probably the best examples are a pair recovered from a bog approximately 20 km west of Edercloon, at Doogarymore, Co. Roscommon (Lucas 1972, 21).

What is most curious about the Edercloon block wheel is that it appears to be unfinished—or rather it could not be finished. The outer curve is not continuous and so this wheel, if completed, would not have been able to roll. This appears to be because the curve was cut too close to the outside of the tree, and there simply was not enough wood to complete it. In addition, there is no evidence of the necessary dowel holes or dowels needed to attach the additional pieces.

Illus. 4—The finely worked surface of the Edercloon block wheel fragment (John Sunderland).

Creative Minds

Illus. 5—A semi-transparent digital reconstruction of the Edercloon block wheel (Chiara Chiriotti, CRDS Ltd).

In order to fully understand the Edercloon wheel and how it might have looked and functioned, it was decided to create a 3D model and hypothetical reconstruction based on similar wheels. Using a scale drawing and carefully recorded measurements, the diameter of the wheel was calculated as 1,200 mm, consistent with many prehistoric block wheels from throughout Europe. The next step in the reconstruction process was the application of texture and colour, carried out with the aid of photographs and a relief map of the worked surface. Finally, additional features such as the transverse dowels and external bracing were added (Illus. 5), the latter features being paralleled on several European examples (Hayen 1987, 214).

From the reconstructed model it was then possible to calculate that the complete wheel, with a volume of 72,541 cm^3, would have been quite heavy at around 40 kg. A large heavy wheel such as this would probably have been used with a similarly heavy and sturdy vehicle, perhaps a cart, and most likely pulled by animals in draught. The early date of the Edercloon block wheel has significant implications for our understanding of early transport in Ireland and possibly also for the use of draught animals.

Prehistoric vehicles are elusive in the archaeological record; however, two probable cart pieces recovered from trackways in counties Longford and Tipperary (Raftery 1996, 273–5;

Taylor 2008, 55) are both of Iron Age date. Although slightly more numerous, yokes are similarly rare; of a small collection of recovered examples, three have been scientifically dated to the Late Bronze Age, while a fourth is suggested on morphological grounds to be of Iron Age date (Stanley et al. 2003). Dating from the Late Bronze Age, the Edercloon wheel indicates that heavy vehicles and draught animals were in use several centuries earlier than these other finds suggest. In addition, contemporary toghers of suitable size (none of the Edercloon trackways could have facilitated wheeled transport) may have been built to accommodate the passage of wheeled vehicles.

Wheel rims and reinvention

Several centuries later at Edercloon a second wheel fragment was deposited. In contrast to the block wheel, which was well buried, this find was in the upper levels of the site and sat in a semi-upright position, in what was a very haphazard section of the trackway. This togher (EDC 12/13) was exceptionally large and had multiple layers, the lowest of which has been dated to 1410–1210 BC (Wk-25202), while the upper layer was dated to 750–390 BC (Wk-25204). The latter date was returned for a piece of hazel brushwood that lay adjacent to the wheel fragment and is believed to have been deposited at the same time.

This find is completely different to the block wheel and appears to have been part of a wheel rim, something like a wooden tyre. Measuring 258 mm long, a maximum of 34 mm wide and 42 mm deep, it is a slightly curved piece of alder, U-shaped in cross-section and broken at both ends (Illus. 6). The upper edge has been carved into a linear groove, which runs along its entire length and is 25 mm wide. Set vertically through this are seven dowel holes, five with dowels *in situ*. These measure 10–15 mm in diameter and most are set in

Illus. 6—The wheel rim fragment and associated dowels from EDC 12/13 (John Sunderland).

Illus. 7—The heavily worn outer surface of the rim fragment from EDC 12/13, with gravel clearly embedded in the dowels (John Sunderland).

pairs, spaced approximately 77 mm apart. The base or rolling surface is heavily striated and worn, and is embedded with tiny fragments of gravel (Illus. 7).

Quite extraordinarily, the only known parallel for this artefact was also recovered at Edercloon but came from EDC 49, a trackway which has been dated to AD 680–880 (Wk-25203). The EDC 49 rim fragment is carved from ash and is much smaller (Illus. 8), measuring only 75 mm long, 30 mm wide and 40 mm deep. Like the EDC 12/13 example, the base is worn and embedded with gravel and sand, the upper surface has the remains of a linear groove and at one end there is a broken dowel hole. Even allowing for the paucity of evidence for the wheel in early Ireland, the recovery at Edercloon of two identical wheel fragments for which there are no parallels, and which appear to date from such dramatically different periods, is truly remarkable. The scientific dating of several other sites at Edercloon has produced results in conflict with the excavated stratigraphy and it seems likely that over the centuries older sites were encountered and exploited for material. Thus it may be that the EDC 49 wheel rim is of significantly earlier date than the trackway within which it was found and is closer in age to that from ECD 12/13. Conversely, it is possible that these two finds represent a local and long-lived tradition of wheel manufacture.

These two finds are believed to be fragments of wheel rims or felloes, which, in contrast to the block wheel, are quite light and finely made and were well used in antiquity. Extensive research on wheels from both Ireland and beyond has thus far failed to find a parallel for these finds and so, using a combination of features from known wheel types and information from the finds themselves, three possible reconstructions have been created.

Being larger, the fragment from EDC 12/13 has provided greater insight into the original size and scale of these wheels, and its shallow curvature indicates an original complete diameter of 800 mm. Given the narrow width of the linear groove, this wheel could not have been thicker than 25 mm, and so would have been much smaller and lighter than the block wheel. One of the first questions raised about these finds concerned the function of the dowels and whether they were in fact the remains of spokes. Spoked wheels

Illus. 8—The small wheel rim fragment from EDC 49, with gravel in the outer surface (John Sunderland).

do not appear to have arrived in western Europe until the Late Bronze Age (Piggott 1983, 110), and did not become common until the Iron Age (Hayen 1987, 214; Mallory 2004, 136). Furthermore, there is no direct evidence for their use in Ireland during this period, although a possible spoke was recovered from a Late Bronze Age togher at Derryfada, Co. Tipperary (Buckley et al. 2005, 316).

Taking the EDC 12/13 rim fragment, with each spoke represented by a dowel, the proposed 800 mm wheel would have had 40 spokes. Measuring only 10–15 mm in diameter, these would have been extremely thin and much too weak to support the weight of a vehicle. As stated above, however, the dowels in this find appear to be set in pairs, and so perhaps each pair was used to secure a stronger spoke. The resulting reconstruction is of a 20-spoke wheel, the spokes of which have expanded terminals secured to the rim with pairs of dowels (Illus. 9). For this arrangement to work, the rim would have to have been made in several pieces, but as both artefacts are incomplete the exact size and number of pieces are unknown. No comparison for this reconstruction was known until recently, when a photo was found of a cartwheel excavated at Tchoga Zanbil, near Susa, south-west Iran, dating from the second millennium BC and currently on display at the National Museum of Iran, Tehran (see http://en.wikipedia.org/wiki/Wheel, accessed November 2009). The spokes of this wheel are very similar to those hypothesised for the Edercloon wheel, with the exception that they are set alternately with the expanded terminals in line with and perpendicular to the felloe.

A second hypothesis as to how the Edercloon wheel rim fragments may have functioned is presented in Illus. 10. This reconstruction is based on one produced for the remains of a chariot dated to the sixth century BC excavated at Ca'Morta, Como, Italy, which

Creative Minds

*Illus. 9—
Reconstruction of a
wheel with spokes
and a segmented
rim or felloe
(Chiara Chiriotti,
CRDS Ltd).*

*Illus. 10—
Reconstruction of a
wheel with short spokes,
wide felloes and a
separate segmented rim
(Chiara Chiriotti,
CRDS Ltd).*

Illus. 11—The proposed hybrid of a block wheel with a separate, segmented rim dowelled in position (Chiara Chiriotti, CRDS Ltd).

comprised four wheels with short, bronze spokes and outer iron rims or tyres (Piggott 1983, 182–4). The reconstruction produced here (Illus. 10) combines short wooden spokes with wide, segmented felloes encircled by a segmented rim which is dowelled in position.

A new hybrid

Individually the three wheel fragments from Edercloon appear to represent two very different traditions of wheel-making, although a final hypothesis brings together both types. This reconstruction (Illus. 11) represents a lighter version of the block wheel, the diameter of which has been reduced to 800 mm and around the edges of which are segments of a wooden rim, dowelled in position. In this hypothesis 40 dowels in the reconstructed rim would appear to be adequate to connect the outer and inner parts of the wheel. The advantage of this wheel would have been the relatively easy replacement of the outer segments in the event of damage. It is important to note that dating evidence and the size of the recovered finds do not suggest that these two elements were ever associated at Edercloon, but the model is a good hypothesis for the use of the wheel rim fragment and its associated dowels. Furthermore, such an arrangement was suggested by wheelwright and traditional carriage-builder Tom Cullinane, who, along with Paddy Egan of Ballymote Carriage Works, examined the find.

Conclusions

That the Edercloon excavations should have produced such diverse and unparalleled evidence for the early wheel in Ireland is extraordinary. Even more curious is the fact that none of the trackways from which these artefacts were recovered were suited to the use of wheeled vehicles. The broad chronological span of these finds points not only to a local tradition of wheel manufacture but also to the enduring tradition of artefact deposition at the site. Like the wheels themselves, this practice originated in the prehistoric period but continued for many centuries. Reinventing the Edercloon wheels through 3D reconstructions has been a fascinating process, and it is hoped that future finds and evidence may yet come to light and so further enhance our understanding of these rare and intriguing artefacts.

Acknowledgements

The authors would like to thank the NRA for the opportunity to participate in the seminar and to contribute to this publication. Many thanks to CRDS Ltd, and in particular to David J O'Connor and Milica Rajic. Sincere thanks to Conor McDermott, Dr Robert Sands and Dr Aidan O'Sullivan of the School of Archaeology, University College Dublin, who have advised, commented and contributed to research on the Edercloon wheels. We are also grateful for the advice of Paddy Egan of Ballymote Carriage Works and to Tom Cullinane. Finally, thanks to the many people who participated in the Edercloon excavations.

Note

1. NGR 206861, 285027; height 25 m OD; excavation reg. no. E3313; ministerial direction no. A031; excavation director Caitríona Moore.

6. Iron-smelting and smithing: new evidence emerging on Irish road schemes

Angela Wallace and Lorna Anguilano

Illus. 1—The stone-lined furnace pit at Tonybaun, Co. Mayo (Mayo County Council).

Iron was of fundamental importance to the economy and lifestyle of Iron Age and later communities. Increasing examination of and analytical work on metallurgical residues, or waste products, from iron-working and associated features from recent archaeological excavations is opening up a whole new area of knowledge concerning early technology in Ireland. There are still many questions to be answered about the origins and development of iron-working. The appearance in Ireland of Continental-type artefacts linked with iron-working communities in mainland Europe is seen as an early indicator of the arrival of iron technology. New archaeological evidence for early iron-smelting sites is now providing fascinating glimpses of the techniques being used by the first iron craft-workers in Ireland.

The similarity or variation in the iron-working evidence across Europe can provide clues as to whether technology spread or was locally developed. The recent discovery of early iron-working furnaces on Irish road schemes with date ranges of 800–400 BC is highly significant in understanding the introduction of the complex craft of iron-smelting into Ireland. The technology is traditionally associated with the arrival of new people as opposed to independent local invention. Further in-depth study is required to determine whether local innovation or foreign influence was behind the early introduction of iron-smelting technology.

Examination of the waste products or slags associated with iron-working and related features from three different iron-working sites discovered on national road schemes are briefly described in this paper in order to illustrate the results being obtained from routine examination and analysis.

Iron production

Locating and processing the ore

Iron ores are rocks and minerals from which metallic iron can be extracted. They are usually composed of minerals rich in iron oxides and vary in colour from dark grey to rusty red. The more common iron-bearing minerals are magnetite, hematite, limonite or siderite. Iron-rich ores are very visible, owing to their colour, but locating and following them would have required a good knowledge of the local landscape and geology. It is widely believed that bog iron ore, formed by the precipitation of iron compounds in lakes and bogs (McDonnell 1995, 1), was the most common ore source used in Ireland, although further research is needed to confirm this. Chemical analysis of slags found on archaeological sites in conjunction with analysis of possible ore sources can help to pinpoint the ores used.

The ore may have been dressed, washed and winnowed to separate out poorer parts and other rocks associated with it, then crushed to a suitably small size to be successfully smelted (see below). This processing may have taken place where the ore was retrieved or at a smelting site elsewhere.

Smelting the processed/unprocessed ore

The smelting process is the most complex step of iron production and there are many variations in the archaeological record regarding smelting methods. Before the development of the blast furnace in the 19th century it was not possible to obtain temperatures high enough to melt iron, so refining was carried out while the material was in a solid or semi-solid state; thus iron-smelting was carried out using the 'direct' or 'bloomery' process. This required a furnace and large quantities of fuel (normally charcoal). It was initially thought that smelting in Ireland was generally carried out in simple bowl furnaces with a low superstructure (Scott 1990, 159); it is likely, however, that many of these furnaces had some sort of clay superstructure in the form of a shaft (see Carlin 2008, 92).

The basic furnace was probably a cylindrical clay shaft 1–2 m in height, with an internal diameter of 0.3–1 m. The walls were normally over 0.2 m thick to reduce heat loss (McDonnell 1995, 1). Often the only remnants of the shaft are fragments of baked clay around the base. The furnace shaft was usually constructed over a shallow pit. The walls may have incorporated preformed clay blocks with tubular openings or tuyères to facilitate blasts of air into the furnace using a bellows; tuyères are also frequently linked to smithing hearths (see below). Temperatures would have been very high around the air inlet, and the tuyères, possibly containing crushed quartz, would have been heat-resistant, preventing them from melting and collapsing during the firing of the furnace/hearth.

The furnace was charged with fuel and preheated. When hot, mixtures of ore and charcoal would be fed into it and bellows used to pump air in. Temperatures would have ranged from initial reduction of the ore at around 800° C high up in the furnace to slag liquation at over 1,000° C near the base (ibid.).

The ores were reduced and broken up by reaction with the burning charcoal, leading to the formation of an iron bloom (a spongy mass of metallic iron mixed with slag impurities) and liquid slag (Carlin 2008, 91). The base of the shaft is likely to have been broken open to retrieve the bloom and rake out the slag; the furnace may have been patched up and reused.

Primary smithing or bloom-processing
The bloom would have been left unmelted, with slag retained in small holes in its spongy texture. To expel the slag a smith would have to hammer the lump on an anvil while the slag was still molten. This would force out the liquid slag, leaving behind fairly pure iron. This was a very difficult, dangerous activity, requiring time, energy and fuel. The bloom might have to be reheated several times to re-melt the slag until the last of it had gone. A smith could eventually produce a block of reasonably pure iron, called wrought iron.

Secondary smithing or artefact-forging
A relatively pure ingot of iron would then have been reheated and forged into an artefact. Smithing can be done anywhere, even at a domestic hearth; it does not need a purpose-built structure. Archaeological evidence for smithing hearths is very poor owing to their position above ground. The smith required fuel and an air blast to obtain high temperatures. By heating the iron the smith increased the chances of it oxidising and becoming useless. This could be avoided by careful control of the fire and also by fluxing the metal surface with sand. Fluxing formed a thin slag layer that cleaned the metal surface and prevented oxidation.

This process produced smithing slags, the most characteristic being plano-convex smithing hearth bottoms or cakes. The hammering of the iron also scattered 'hammerscale', the oxidised film of metal from the surface, around the working area. Hammerscale and anvil stones, along with the plano-convex hearth bottoms and amorphous smithing slag lumps, are the most diagnostic finds on an excavation associated with a smithing hearth.

Early iron-working

The availability in recent years of a wide range of dates from iron-working hearths and furnaces suggests that the earliest evidence for actual iron-working in Ireland dates from around 800–400 BC. This date range is based on two sites excavated on the M4 Kinnegad–Enfield–Kilcock motorway scheme, namely Rossan 6, Co. Meath, and Kinnegad 2, Co. Westmeath (Carlin 2008, 88, 105). There are, however, some difficulties with the date ranges obtained from iron-working furnaces and features, as oak charcoal was most commonly used as fuel; oak trees can live for 300–400 years and the use of old oak can create dating problems (ibid.; Warner 1990).

The use of statistical analysis for radiocarbon dates obtained from charcoal associated with furnaces, along with other techniques such as archaeomagnetic dating (based on the magnetisation of material heated in the past fossilising the direction and strength of the Earth's magnetic field at that time) and thermoluminescence dating (based on determining the last time a crystal within fired clay was heated and electrons released), may prove more useful in obtaining tighter date ranges for the earliest iron-working sites. Archaeomagnetic dating is particularly suitable for soils subjected to high temperatures, such as those found in hearths and furnaces, and proved useful in obtaining narrower date ranges for prehistoric iron-working furnaces found at the Bryn y Castell hillfort in north-west Wales (Crew 1986, 98). This can only be carried out while excavation is ongoing, however, and will apply only to sites found on future developments. Thermoluminescence dating is an emerging technique for dating metallurgical material and an experimental study in Germany on metallurgical residues from various sites with reference data has shown promising results (Haustein et al. 2003). Reliable dating and examination of the iron-working sites yielding the earliest dates are crucial in developing an understanding of how technology was introduced and developed in Ireland.

One such early site was identified at Tonybaun, 6 km south of Ballina, Co. Mayo, during the excavation of a children's burial ground in advance of the construction of the N26 Ballina to Bohola (Stage 1) road scheme. This site was excavated in 2003 by Joanna Nolan of Mayo County Council on behalf of the NRA.[1] Several metal-working features predating the 15th–20th-century burial ground were identified during the excavation, and 31.85 kg of iron slag and associated residues were recovered in association with various iron-working features (Nolan 2006). A single stone-lined pit, believed to be the remains of a smelting furnace, with 18.45 kg of associated smelting residues, was dated to 477–210 BC (UB-6765; see Appendix 1 for details) and represents one of the earliest dated iron-smelting pits from the west of Ireland.

The early furnace pit at Tonybaun consisted of a small, rounded, stone-lined pit; examination of associated residues indicated that it was used for smelting iron ore. The stone lining was unusual as most excavated furnaces are unlined. It is likely that there was originally a low, clay shaft superstructure over this pit. The pit measured 0.91 m by 0.89 m and 0.29 m in depth. Five stone slabs were set upright around the sides, and at the base was a small square slab. All of the stones were fire-cracked and gaps between the uprights were filled with a very fine-grained silt or daub-like clay. The fill consisted of almost pure charcoal, mixed with flecks of topsoil and 18.45 kg of slag (Illus. 1).

The morphology of the Tonybaun furnace is so far unique in an Irish context. Some stone-lined and partly lined furnaces are known from north and central European contexts, but they vary greatly in depth and dating evidence varies widely (Pleiner 2000, 144). There is one small, stone-lined pit from Austria dated to the fifth century BC (ibid.) that is broadly similar to that at Tonybaun, and several stone-lined Iron Age furnaces were excavated at Culduthel Farm, Inverness, Scotland (Murray 2008), which points to links in the spread and development of these early types of iron-smelting furnaces.

A smithing area consisting of a large boulder (probably used as an anvil) surrounded by a layer of charcoal and associated smithing slags was also identified at Tonybaun, c. 17 m north-east of the furnace pit. This area was dated to 166 BC–AD 25 (UB-6763), which may suggest that the furnace date has been distorted by the 'old wood effect'. The overall evidence from examination of the metallurgical assemblage points to a small-scale production site, where iron ore was smelted and the resulting bloom was worked to remove slag impurities and then reworked to produce an artefact or several artefacts. The early date of iron-working features from this site must be treated with caution but is nevertheless highly significant in terms of the evolution of early iron technology in Ireland.

A total of 5.37 kg of residues was associated with a pit interpreted as a possible bloom-smithing hearth at Rossan 6, Co. Meath, but this interpretation is problematic. Oak charcoal from this feature produced a very early radiocarbon date of 820–780 BC (Beta-177434) but, owing to the old wood effect, the hearth may be up to 300 years later in date. The metallurgical specialist who examined the residues proposed that the pit 'originally served as a charcoaling platform or in some other capacity and [was] subsequently converted to a bloom smithing hearth' (Photos-Jones 2008a, 10). Several fragments of vitrified clay and a single piece of porous slag were recovered from this pit, but this material may have been dumped here from elsewhere and it is questionable whether a single piece of slag is definitive evidence for an iron bloom-smithing hearth. A later date of 370–50 BC (Beta-177435) was obtained from a bowl furnace with associated smelting slags (ibid., 14); this would seem to be a more reliable and plausible date for the small-scale iron-working activity on this site.

The potential metal-working feature from Kinnegad 2, Co. Westmeath, dated to 810–420 BC (Beta-177427), also has quite weak links with actual iron-working; it is described as a clay-filled spread 'more likely to have been a hearth, perhaps domestic, in which slag from later activities was dumped' (Photos-Jones 2008b, 4). A date of 400–210 BC (Beta-177428) was obtained from a deposit associated with a bowl furnace at Kinnegad 2, and again it seems that the fifth- to third-century BC date is the most plausible.

A pit interpreted as a bowl furnace (Photos-Jones 2008c, 9) was excavated at Johnstown 3, Co. Meath, also on the M4 KEK, and produced a date of 420–230 BC (Beta-177442). This date, which is roughly contemporary with the Tonybaun furnace, appears to be reliable, although there is no available information on the type and quantity of metallurgical residues from the furnace. The combined evidence from Tonybaun, Rossan 6, Kinnegad 2 and Johnstown 3 suggests that the first iron-working in Ireland is likely to have developed towards the late fifth or early fourth century BC. Additional confirmation of this has come from Newrath, Co. Kilkenny (N25 Waterford City Bypass), and from Curraheen 1 (N22 Ballincollig Bypass), Transtown AR29 (N8 Glanmire–Watergrasshill Bypass) and Lisnagar Demesne 1 (M8 Rathcormac/Fermoy Bypass) in County Cork (see Appendix 1). The problems with using oak charcoal from these early furnaces need to be looked at closely, as the 'old wood effect' throws considerable doubt over all the early dates. In order to establish a more reliable chronology, it may be necessary in the future to use radiocarbon dates in conjunction with other techniques (e.g. archaeomagnetic and thermoluminescence dating).

Early medieval iron-working

Many of the large assemblages of iron slag recovered from excavations on road schemes are associated with early and high medieval sites, when iron-working became more organised and widespread among rural settlements. There is much variation in the volume of iron slags recovered from early medieval sites; assemblages usually range from 30 kg to 200 kg, although there are some exceptional sites with assemblages weighing over 1 tonne. These are particularly interesting in documenting the level of organisation for large-scale production, although it is often difficult to determine the duration of activity on these sites. Johnstown 1, Co. Meath, a multiperiod cemetery-settlement, yielded over 2 tonnes of iron-smelting and smithing waste, and dating evidence suggests that iron-working took place here over several centuries (Clarke & Carlin 2008, 75). Clonfad, Co. Westmeath, a monastic site dated to between the sixth and ninth centuries AD (see Chapter 7), produced up to 1.5

Creative Minds

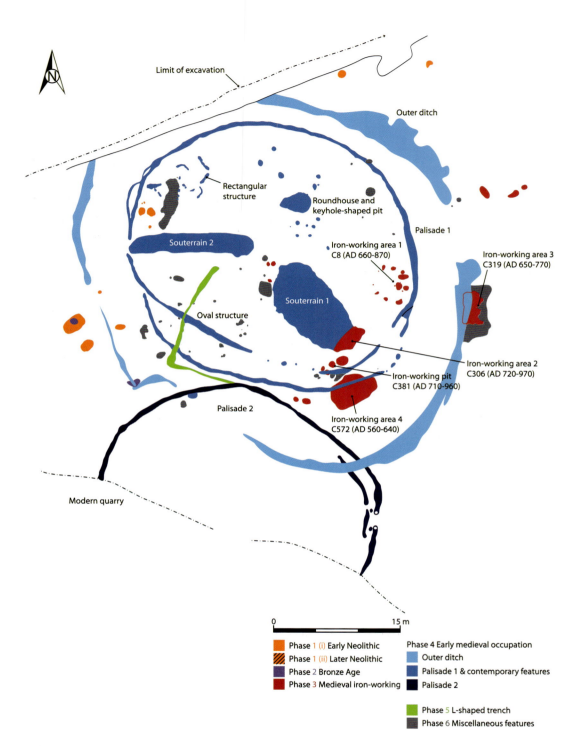

Illus. 2—Plan of the multiphase settlement site at Lowpark, Co. Mayo, showing the location and dating of the early medieval iron-working features (Mayo County Council).

tonnes of smithing waste; this site functioned as a larger, more specialised site for the production of iron hand-bells (Stevens 2006; 2007c).

Lowpark, Co. Mayo

In 2005 a multiperiod settlement enclosure was excavated at Lowpark, Co. Mayo, on the N5 Charlestown Bypass, by Richard Gillespie of Mayo County Council on behalf of the NRA.[2] The site produced 1,364.50 kg of metallurgical waste (Gillespie & Kerrigan, forthcoming). Residues were recovered from various features on the site, and four clearly defined iron-working areas were identified. These represented separate smithing workshops (Illus. 2) and produced a date range spanning the sixth to the 10th centuries AD (see Appendix 1). Hearths and pits within these areas varied considerably in morphology; basal rims of clay superstructures were noted in association with some of the hearths, and large quantities of baked clay fragments suggested substantial superstructures. Three tuyère fragments were also recovered, indicating substantial, well-insulated smithing hearths with clay walls and blow-holes for the use of bellows.

Three of the iron-working areas were within sunken subrectangular structures (Illus. 3); the fourth workshop (iron-working area 3) was located within a partly silted-up enclosure ditch. The presence of an iron-working area within or associated with an enclosure ditch appears to be a recurring phenomenon on other enclosure sites. At Rathgall, Co. Wicklow, a furnace was dug into the top of a silted-up later Bronze Age ditch, and at Clogher, Co. Tyrone, excavation of part of an Iron Age ditch revealed a smelting and smithing complex (Scott 1990, 160). A smithing area at the Hiberno-Scandinavian site at Woodstown, Co. Waterford, was also located in a ditch (O'Brien et al. 2005, 75).

Illus. 3—Iron-working area 4, one of the sunken smithing workshops excavated at Lowpark (Mayo County Council).

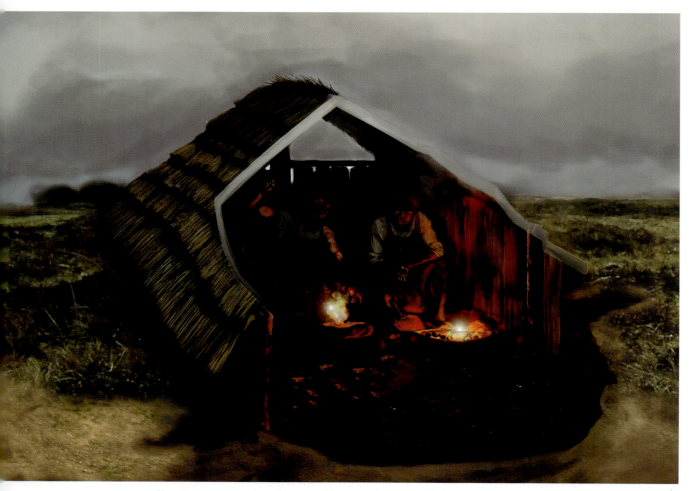

Illus. 4—Reconstruction of iron-working area 4 at Lowpark (Fergus Niland).

The deliberate sunken areas at Lowpark may have had a functional purpose, providing better insulation for the hearths. In addition, if the area was well sheltered it would be easier to control the airflow within the hearths, and darkened areas were often used by smiths as the colour of the heated metal and the flame indicated readiness for welding or hammering (Illus. 4).

The slags discovered at Lowpark were identified as mainly smithing slags owing to their morphology of mostly rounded cakes, although there were also many small amorphous fragments or smithing slag lumps. Smithing slag cakes can be plano-convex, concave-convex or convex-convex in profile. They are usually subcircular in plan; their size and weight can vary considerably from 100 g to more than 2 kg, but the majority weigh 200–500 g.

As a generalisation, slag cakes from the refining of iron blooms will be larger and heavier than those from secondary smithing, but much depends on the amount of iron forged, how much slag it contained, whether fluxes were used and how often the hearth was cleaned out (Crew 1996).

Most of the slags from Lowpark were plano-convex and concave-convex in profile (Illus. 5), common shapes for smithing slags formed in a hearth. Some of the samples taken

Illus. 5—Cross-section through a concave-convex smithing hearth cake from Lowpark (Lorna Anguilano).

from the slag had evidence for two phases of smithing activity, one on top of the other. The weight of the more complete slag cakes, at around 1 kg, indicates a long period of activity. Smithing of larger or complex artefacts would require different techniques, longer episodes of activity and subsequently larger hearth cakes, with evidence for phases of activity in cross-section.

Microscopic examination and bulk chemical analysis were carried out on 12 subsamples from smithing slags from Lowpark. In general, iron slags consist mainly of iron oxide, alumina and silica. Vast quantities of iron are lost in the smelting and smithing process. The alumina and silica come from the surrounding clay in the hearth and from sand or clay used as a flux; the chemical composition of the fuel used also contributes to the chemistry of the slag.

The slags would also contain trace quantities of phosphorus, manganese, potassium, sodium, calcium and titanium. The trace elements can help in identifying whether a single or a variety of ore sources or types were being used. Using a scanning electron microscope (which gives very high-powered magnification in conjunction with an analytical device for determining the chemical make-up of the material), different mineral phases within the slag were selected and analysed. There was very little variation between the area analyses obtained within each of the Lowpark samples. The slag material was quite homogeneous in chemical composition, suggesting the use of a single ore source. There was, however, evidence for variation between the samples from the top and bottom portion of each slag cake. This variation is considered important as it is indicative of a change in smithing activity within the cycle that produced each slag cake.

The chemical composition of the samples was mainly characterised by the presence of

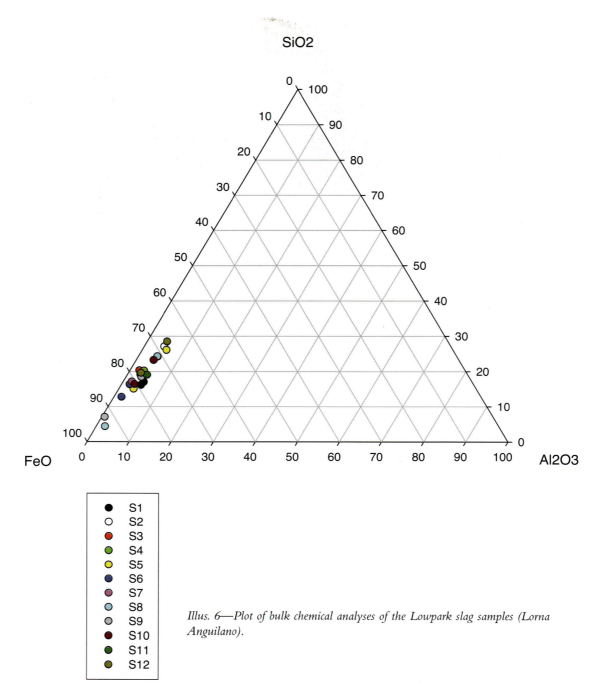

Illus. 6—Plot of bulk chemical analyses of the Lowpark slag samples (Lorna Anguilano).

iron oxide concentrations of between 70% and 90% (Illus. 6), pointing to a temperature of 1,100–1,200° C within the smithing hearth. Some of the samples are rich in iron while others have a higher than usual concentration of silica. The iron-rich material is mainly produced by loss of metallic particles while forging a poorly compacted metal. It can also occur when the smith is working with a temperature near to the melting point of the metal, possibly during welding operations after the manufacture of an object at the end of the iron-processing cycle. The silica-rich material characterising the subsamples from the upper portion of some of the slag cakes is produced when the smith adds a large quantity of flux to the surface of the metal.

The melting point of iron is 1,538° C but it was not possible for early medieval smiths to create temperatures sufficient to melt iron; they therefore worked it in a semi-solid state. The use of a flux on the surface of the metal helped to reduce the melting point so that the smith would have been working at temperatures of 1,100–1,200° C.

Finally, after the fashioning of an object was completed, sand was applied to minimise oxidation, which would produce loss of metal and degradation of the surface.

Analysis of some clay lining used in the hearths showed a composition very rich in silica (average of 80% weight), quartz being the main natural source of silica. Angular quartz grains were visible in the clay matrix when viewed through a microscope (Illus. 7) and indicated the deliberate addition of crushed quartz as a temper to the clay. Quartz would have been added to the clay lining in order to make the clay more refractory or heat-resistant—the melting point of quartz is 1,670° C.

Illus. 7—Angular quartz grains visible within clay matrix of hearth lining (Lorna Anguilano).

Many large early medieval enclosure sites that have produced evidence for iron-working activity have been excavated around the country. None have produced comparable evidence of clearly defined sunken areas used specifically for iron-working in conjunction with such a large volume of metallurgical material. The analysis of samples from the Lowpark slags has highlighted the possibility that certain phases within smithing slags can be closely linked to certain stages within the smithing process. The iron-rich material identified in some slag samples may come from the last stage of consolidating an iron bloom (squeezing out slag impurities through alternate cycles of hammering and heating), or could also be linked to welding operations, which would represent the end of the manufacturing cycle. Hammerscale formed during bloom consolidation would be scattered around the smithing area or become part of the smithing slag cake, forming iron-rich levels in the slag. The artefactual evidence points to the production and repair or recycling of small-scale everyday artefacts such as knives, nails, buckles and shears (Illus. 8).

The large slag cakes at Lowpark suggest that the refining and consolidating of iron blooms and the production of iron bars (raw material for manufacturing) took place here. Further screening of some of the heavier cakes using X-ray technology or radiography may reveal the presence of iron blooms from the site. The large quantity of material, along with the different mineral and chemical phases identified within the Lowpark slag cakes, provides

Creative Minds

Illus. 8—A selection of iron knives recovered from Lowpark (Jonathan Hession).

important evidence of increasing levels of technological complexity and the demarcation of industrial activities within domestic settlement areas towards the end of the Iron Age and into the early medieval period.

The differentiation of the activities (tool repair, bloom consolidation, artefact manufacture, etc.) in different areas of the workshop/different workshops indicates division of the work between specialised craftsmen. There are indications of organisation of the space into activity-focused areas possibly furnished with activity-focused tools.

Borris, Co. Tipperary
Excavation of a medieval site (AR33) in Borris townland, just outside the village of Twomileborris, Co. Tipperary, in advance of the construction of the M8/N8 Cullahill–Cashel road scheme, yielded an assemblage of 142.74 kg of iron slag from a metalworking area including two furnaces and three smithing hearths (Ó Droma 2008, 57). The site was excavated by Mícheál Ó Droma of Valerie J Keeley Ltd on behalf of Kilkenny County Council and the NRA.[3] This assemblage consisted mainly of iron-smithing slag in the form of smithing hearth cakes, slag lumps and by-products such as hammerscale. Approximately 80–100 smithing hearth cakes (30–40% of the assemblage) were identified, ranging from 0.2 kg to 1.3 kg in weight (the average is approximately 0.57 kg). A large proportion (c. 60%) of the material from the site consists of smithing slag lumps. Fragments of furnace lining and one possible tuyère fragment were also identified.

The most significant find from Borris was a well-preserved, partly compacted loaf-shaped or rounded iron bloom weighing 3 kg (Illus. 9); very few consolidated blooms have

Illus. 9—Partly compacted, loaf-shaped iron bloom from site AR33, Borris, Co. Tipperary, prior to sectioning (Angela Wallace).

been documented previously in Ireland. Blooms can only be identified positively using radiography or sectioning and sampling of material. As it has only become routine in recent years for detailed specialist reports to be compiled on metallurgical residues, there is a strong likelihood that more blooms will be identified from Irish sites through consistent screening and radiography or sampling of material.

The bloom was recovered from the uppermost fill of a circular pit located c. 12 m northwest of a smithing hearth dated to AD 680–774 (UBA-12501). Features in the vicinity of this pit date from the seventh to the 12th century and thus it is not possible to date the bloom with certainty (P Stevens, pers. comm.). From the surface the rounded bloom appeared almost identical to an iron smithing cake and it was only after sectioning that it was identified (Illus. 10).

The bloom has a very regular circular shape; it is 130 mm in diameter and 60 mm thick. The sample was cut in two halves and a slice was taken from the centre in order to carry out detailed analyses on the chemical and structural composition of the metal. Microscopic observation indicated the presence of slag associated with iron metal and the coalescence of iron metal through the slag in a solid reaction typical of bloomery smelting (Illus. 11). The composition of the slag agrees well with the compositional analyses of the smithing

Illus. 10—Loaf-shaped bloom after sectioning, showing iron metal mixed with slag impurities (Lorna Anguilano).

slags from the site, indicating a strong correlation between the recovered materials.

The regular rounded shape of the Borris bloom is morphologically comparable with three loaf-shaped blooms (2.45–3.2 kg) from a 10th-century smelting site at Somogyfajsz, southern Hungary; another bloom of this type (3.1 kg) was also recovered from a 10th–11th-century context in western Moravia (Pleiner 2000, 236–7). There is a 13th-century unforged example (6.4 kg) from Downpatrick, Co. Down (Tylecote 1977), and a loaf-shaped bloom from the 13th-century phase of the large urban site at Novgorod, northern Russia, which appears to be very similar to that from Borris (Pleiner 2000, 236–7).

The evidence from Borris points to small-scale primary and secondary smithing. The presence of the partly consolidated iron bloom proves that this type of iron was probably being traded to early medieval farmsteads to be worked up into everyday artefacts, indicating that primary and secondary smithing were performed separately at specialised sites.

Artefacts recovered from this site include over 30 fragments of miscellaneous iron objects or pieces of scrap iron, several iron nails, tanged iron knives, blades, an iron ring-pin, a pin and an iron chain. This provides some clues as to the type of artefacts likely to have been manufactured and repaired here.

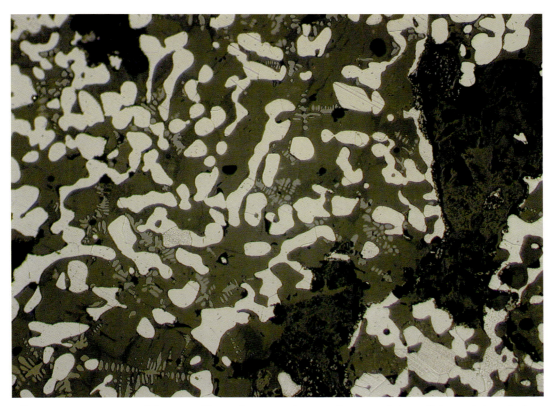

Illus. 11—Microstructure of the Borris bloom, showing coalescence of iron metal drops (light grey) through the slag (dark grey) (Lorna Anguilano).

Conclusions

Very little ore has been positively identified from excavations, perhaps because of difficulties in distinguishing it from other residues recovered. There is a distinct lack of large-scale iron-smelting sites within the archaeological record. Smelting probably took place close to the source of the iron ore or to the source of the fuel so as to avoid the transportation of large quantities of ore/fuel. It is likely that charcoal kilns would be located in close proximity to smelting sites.

A programme of research using 18th- and 19th-century mining records, along with geological and environmental data for iron mineral deposits and bog ore sources, backed up with fieldwork and survey may lead to the discovery of Iron Age and early historic mining and smelting sites. The prehistoric copper mines of Mount Gabriel and Ross Island, Co. Cork, were initially recognised during the development of 19th-century mining industries, observations from which were later used by archaeologists to positively identify early copper-mining (O'Brien 1996, 14–15). The use of experimental archaeology to reconstruct hearths and furnaces in the style of those found on excavations and attempts to source similar raw materials to those used could also help to develop and test hypotheses about how technology was being used.

The evidence emerging so far from recently excavated sites on national road schemes indicates small-scale smelting and smithing on Iron Age sites. Further research is required on the early sites and associated residues to obtain a clearer understanding of the development and adoption of early iron-working technology in Ireland. Caution must be exercised in the overreliance on radiocarbon dating; a combination of dating methods will be needed to provide definitive dates for the earliest smelting sites.

Evidence from early medieval sites indicates that a majority of rural sites practised small-scale smelting and smithing, while large-scale production sites such as Clonfad and Lowpark may have specialised in smithing (with the exception of Johnstown 1, which had evidence for both smelting and smithing on a large scale).

The evidence points to the increasing specialisation of iron-working activities in the early medieval period, with the different iron-working stages being carried out at different sites. It seems that blooms from smelting were transported to workshops often associated with settlement enclosures and then reheated and hammered to further refine and shape them into iron bars that would be traded further afield for manufacture into artefacts. The presence of a loaf-shaped, partly consolidated bloom at Borris is an important discovery and provides further evidence that various stages in the smithing process were being carried out at specific sites during the medieval period. The analytical data are providing more clues regarding the specific stages of iron-working that took place on various sites and also within specific workshops on the same site.

Acknowledgements

Thanks to Richard Gillespie, Joanna Nolan, Gerry Walsh and Gary Burke, all archaeologists with Mayo County Council, and Mícheál Ó Droma and Paul Stevens of Valerie J Keeley Ltd.

Notes

1. Tonybaun, Co. Mayo: NGR 124790, 312310; height 20 m OD; excavation licence no. 03E0139; RMP no. MA039-107.
2. Lowpark, Co. Mayo: NGR 147233, 300643; height 84 m OD; excavation reg. no. E3338; ministerial direction no. A020.
3. Borris (Site AR33), Co. Tipperary: NGR 219538, 157496; height 113–117 m OD; excavation reg. no E2376; ministerial direction no. A027.

7. For whom the bell tolls: the monastic site at Clonfad 3, Co. Westmeath

Paul Stevens

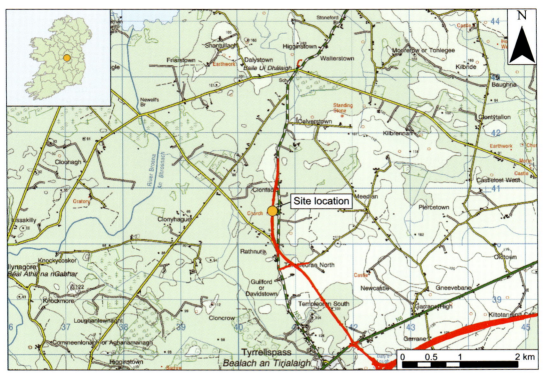

Illus. 1—Location of site at Clonfad, Co. Westmeath (based on the Ordnance Survey Ireland map).

Clonfad 3 is located in rolling fertile countryside south of Lough Ennell, Co. Westmeath (Illus. 1), which historically formed the western border of the ancient kingdom of Mide. The site sits on a slight elevation, an elongated esker hillock that is reflected in the townland and parish placename *Clúain Fóta Fine*, meaning 'long meadow'. To the west is an expansive, low-lying marshland leading to the River Brosna (Illus. 2). Archaeological excavation at Clonfad took place on the south-eastern slopes of the hillock, close to a shallow drainage ditch and field boundary hedge that ran east to west around the excavation area. A small stream or brook, diverted in modern times, flows through the ditch. The old course of the stream had a steep scarp slope preserved along its northern bank and this forms the southern terminus of the hillock and also the limit of the excavation.

An archaeological excavation on behalf of Westmeath County Council and the NRA took place here from November 2004 to March 2005, in advance of the construction of the N52 link road that formed part of the N6 Kinnegad to Kilbeggan Dual Carriageway.[1] The alignment of the link road at Clonfad sought to avoid a ruined church and graveyard (Record of Monuments and Places No. WM 032-089), and in so doing the new route encountered a previously unknown series of earthwork enclosures (O'Connor et al. 2004).

Creative Minds

Illus. 2—Clonfad excavations from the air, from the east, showing the new road alignment passing the church and graveyard (Valerie J Keeley Ltd).

Illus. 3—Aerial view of Clonfad looking west, showing the suggested line of the early medieval monastic enclosures and the original course of the stream (Valerie J Keeley Ltd).

It is now clear that the church and graveyard represent the core of an early medieval monastery dating from between the sixth and ninth centuries AD, which lay within a large monastic trivallate enclosure (Illus. 3). Geophysical survey beyond the excavation area has shown that the monastery expanded over time to enclose an area of 4.54 ha (Illus. 4). The wider archaeological landscape shows a low level of known settlement in the early medieval period. Two church sites are located in Templeoran North, 1.2 km to the south-east, and Meedian, 1.5 km to the east; the latter was accessed from Clonfad in the last century by a Mass path.

A number of significant features and artefacts were identified at the site, including unique evidence for monastic hand-bell production from one of the largest assemblages of metal-working debris found in Ireland to date. The findings at Clonfad provide the earliest and first direct evidence of the use of brazing in the manufacture of Irish hand-bells—a technique for applying a thin bronze coat to the surface of a bell, making the surface continuous across the joins of the iron sheet used to make it and producing a characteristic acoustic 'ring'. The use of this technique for the application of bronze onto hand-bells was previously unknown and was tested subsequently by experimental reconstruction of the brazing process and the creation of two replica hand-bells, carried out by archaeometallurgist Dr Tim Young, GeoArch Ltd, in a research project co-funded by *Amgueddfa Cymru* National Museum Wales and the NRA (Egan 2009).

Geophysical surveys conducted both before (by IGAS Ltd) and after (by Target Archaeological Geophysics) the excavation showed that enclosing elements associated with the former monastic site survived beyond the excavated area to the north, south, east and west of the ruined stone church and graveyard (Illus. 4). An elongated oval enclosure ditch (the outer enclosure) surrounds the graveyard area and measures 200 m in length (north–south) by 180 m in width. It curves around the 91 m contour, encompassing the summit of the hillock and terminating at the stream. Concentric to this enclosure is a substantial enclosing feature, 140–160 m in diameter, which follows a zigzag line. This may be evidence of terracing events or of several different periods of activity 10–15 m inside the outer enclosure. Within this second enclosed area, numerous pit and ill-defined linear and curvilinear features are evident. A third, small, circular enclosure (the inner enclosure) is also suggested by the geophysical data, encircling the present walled graveyard and measuring 75 m in diameter (Nicholls, forthcoming).

Excavation results

The site was subject to archaeological test-trenching in 2003, which first revealed the potential of the location (O'Connor et al. 2004), and the subsequent full excavation was carried out over an area that measured 170 m in length and 45–50 m in width (Illus. 5). The results identified three distinct periods of archaeological activity, dating from the early medieval to the post-medieval periods, including three phases within the early medieval period, notably 'monastic' activity, which is largely the subject of this paper.

The results highlight the outer precincts of what served as the monastic *valla*—enclosing ramparts dividing the monastery into various precincts where only specific activities (e.g. industry) could be carried out. The richness of the record indicates that much of the monastic site remains undisturbed beyond the road corridor. The early monastic origins of

Creative Minds

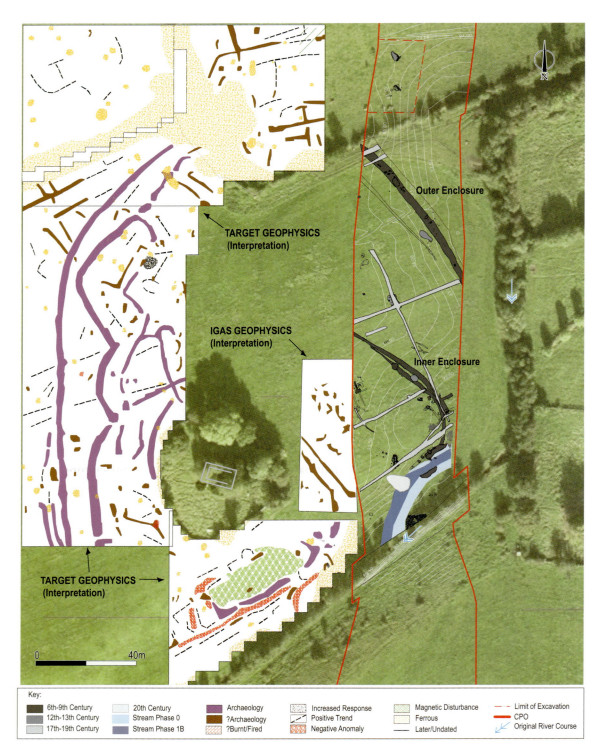

Illus. 4—Vertical aerial view of Clonfad, incorporating a schematic plan of the excavated features, a pre-excavation topographical survey and simplified geophysical survey results (Target Archaeological Geophysics Ltd/IGAS Ltd/Valerie J Keeley Ltd).

Clonfad historically appear to stretch back to the sixth century. It is presumed to have been founded by St Finnian of Clonard, who died in AD 549 (*AFM*, 549; *AU*, 549.3), although the place-name implies that 'Librán, the son of Finna' was the actual founder (Connon, forthcoming). Evidence from the excavation suggested that the monastery survived into the mid- to late ninth century, which is also echoed by historical references to the site being burned in AD 887 (*AFM*, 887; Connon, forthcoming).

Phase 1A (fifth to sixth century AD)
The early monastic site (phase 1A) was evidenced by limited indications of an organised settlement, mostly concentrated close to the stream (and possibly the site of the present church), which subsequently expanded into a large trivallate enclosed settlement. The absence of burial or residential activity within the excavated area and the artefact assemblage was balanced by substantial evidence for metal-working activity. The evidence strongly suggests that it was an industrial sector and supports existing hypotheses regarding the compartmentalisation of activity on monastic sites. The range of metal-working debris showed that highly specialised iron-working took place at this time and continued to be conducted throughout the lifespan of the monastery.

The earliest remains are limited in nature and scale but reflect an early preoccupation with metal-working, including a 1.5-tonne dump of slag residue from large-scale iron-smithing and, in particular, brazing shroud fragments (vitrified clay fragments with impressed circles and lines on one side; see below). This evidence establishes Clonfad as having produced one of the largest and most important early medieval metallurgical assemblages yet identified in Ireland. Linear ditches and pits provide (secondary) evidence of permanent settlement close by. Charred cereal grains, recovered from the linear ditch, show that arable farming was an important part of the local contemporary agriculture.

Phase 1B (seventh to eighth century AD)
During the following stage (phase 1B) of the early medieval activity at Clonfad, the large slag dump impeded the flow of the stream. By the seventh and eighth centuries the early monastery appears to have been reorganised, and the process of defining the monastic precincts with a series of enclosing earthwork ditches and banks took place (Illus. 3 & 4). Large, deep ditches were dug to isolate, encircle and subdivide the area of the monastic precincts. These enclosures are oval or circular in plan and comprised two or three concentric boundaries. Churches were typically located in the central enclosure or in separate enclosures around the site (Edwards 1990, 106–7).

While the excavation necessarily focused on c. 14% of the total area enclosed, the geophysical surveys confirmed the continuation of these enclosing elements around the larger site area (Illus. 4). The outer enclosure ditch has a diameter of 180–200 m and terminates at the stream in the south and south-east quadrant. Excavation showed that it had a V-shaped profile with a narrow but flat base, measuring 2.8–3.4 m wide and 1.8–2.5 m deep. This compares with other medium-sized and large monastic sites of the period, and shows remarkable similarities with Nendrum, Co. Down, Clonmacnoise, Co. Offaly, and Portmahomack, Ross-shire, Scotland (Lawlor 1925; McErlean & Crothers 2007; Murphy 2003; Carver 2008; Stevens, forthcoming).

An internal enclosing ditch (the inner enclosure) was also identified in the centre of the excavation area. The circuit of the ditch commenced at the stream to the south and

Creative Minds

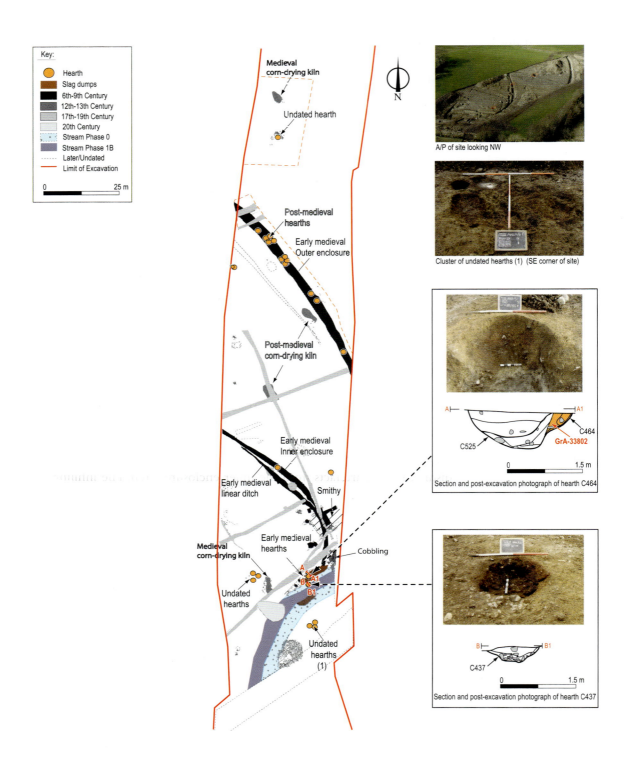

Illus. 5—Site plan showing location of iron-working hearths (all periods) (Valerie J Keeley Ltd).

extended north, curving gently for a radius of c. 60 m and extending beyond the limit of excavation. Charcoal from the silt basal fill of this ditch returned a date of AD 688–878 (UBA-8679; see Appendix 1 for details), confirming a trend for ecclesiastical enclosure in the seventh century, but there is little additional evidence for seventh-century activity within the excavated area. A middle enclosure wall at Nendrum monastery was built during the early medieval phase of that site and several building platforms were built against the enclosure (Lawlor 1925; McErlean & Crothers 2007, 335). The terraced features noted in the geophysical survey at Clonfad may represent similar platforms.

Within the excavation area, the interior between the two enclosure ditches was mostly devoid of archaeological features, except for a small area of cobbling beside the inner enclosure ditch which led down to the stream (Illus. 5). The cobbling may represent a metalled pathway or even a fording place for wheeled traffic, which suggests some comparison with a large metalled road at a contemporary monastery at Portmahomack (Carver 2008). No evidence, however, was observed for a continuation of the cobbling on the south side of the stream and no wheel rutting was noted. In contrast, the space between the stream and the inner enclosure contained a series of wells, pits and smithing hearths (Illus. 5). The activity was focused on the northern bank of the stream, and similar activity further west beyond the excavated area was identified to the south of the church by the geophysical survey (Illus. 4).

The monastic enclosure at Clonfad saw a dramatic reorganisation in the eighth–ninth centuries, and this may have been associated with a contraction of the site. Both enclosures were partly or completely filled in, but the area adjacent to the stream continued in use with evidence of iron-working. This later phase of activity produced much of the artefactual and environmental evidence, reflecting the dump of refuse into the ditches; however, there was a distinct lack of artefacts from the inner enclosure ditch. The infilling of the inner enclosure was matched by similar activity on the outer enclosure, at roughly the same time. Radiocarbon determinations from both ditches suggest that they were infilled in the eighth century (see Appendix 1).

The outer ditch was backfilled in a single episode, shown by the recovery of bone artefact fragments from the lower, middle and upper layers that could be fitted together. Deposits within the backfill also contained copper-alloy artefacts, metal scrap and ingots, ceramic crucible fragments, worked bone objects and manufacturing waste, smithing hearth cakes (see Chapter 6), tuyères (nozzles in a furnace through which air was injected), many ferrous metal objects/tools (nails, a knife blade and a buckle), stone casting moulds and a possible lamp. Fragments of human bone and animal bone refuse were also recovered. The ditch fills produced evidence for the manufacture of antler/bone combs, bone beads (possibly prayer beads), woodworking and leather-working (Illus. 6). This rich collection represented the discarded refuse of several crafts from several workshops (Stevens 2006; forthcoming).

In AD 891 Clonfad is mentioned in the historical annals for the last time: 'Conchobhar, son of Flannagan, lord of Ui Failghe, is destroyed by fire at Clúain-fóta-Fine, in the church; and the relics of Finnian were violated by the Fear Tulach' (*AFM*, 887; see also Connon, forthcoming). While fragmentary historical references are difficult to marry with complex archaeological evidence, there is a complete lack of archaeological evidence for activity at the site after the ninth century. Whether the monastery was destroyed and completely abandoned following this event cannot be conclusively determined based on the limited

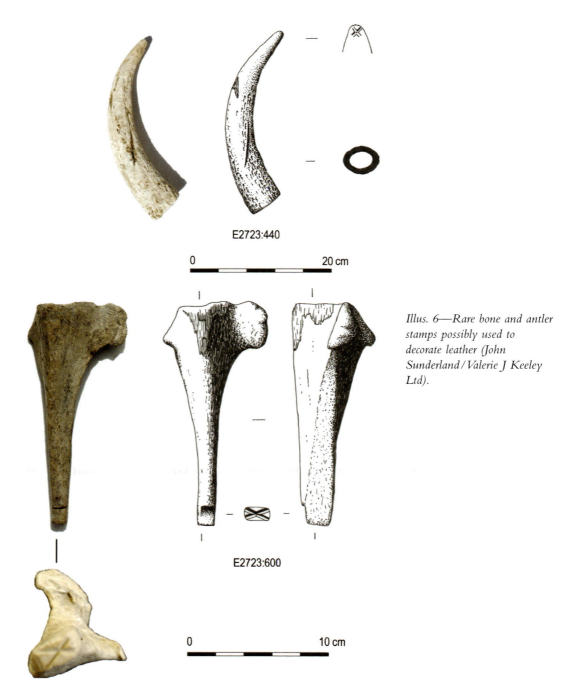

Illus. 6—Rare bone and antler stamps possibly used to decorate leather (John Sunderland/Valerie J Keeley Ltd).

evidence. Nevertheless, it is clear that the main iron-working industry of the monastery was discontinued by the late ninth or early 10th century.

Later phases

Later activity at the site was evidenced by agriculture during the 12th–13th centuries (phase 2) and included two cereal-drying kilns (Illus. 5). Historically a parish church at Clonfad is known to have continued in use throughout the second millennium and the ruined stone church may date from this phase. Phase 3, related to agricultural reorganisation and small-scale iron-smithing in the 17th–19th centuries, was associated with an adjacent vernacular dwelling, immediately west of the area of excavation. Several linear drainage ditches, two stone-lined cereal-drying kilns, smithing hearths, landscaping features such as tree plantation pits and field boundary ditches are associated with this later activity. Undated features uncovered by the excavation include a juvenile inhumation, pits, ditches and hearths.

Metallurgical residues

The most common and prolific activity at Clonfad was iron-working (Illus. 5). The majority of the metal-working evidence related to primary and secondary smithing waste (see Chapter 6), with evidence for smelting being almost completely absent. Smelting of the raw iron ore material may have been carried out elsewhere, probably locally. Metal-working residues (slag) are commonly found in small volumes on early medieval sites, though the very large assemblage recovered at Clonfad is unusual. Tuyères and smithing hearths and furnaces are known from many sites, such as Nendrum, Co. Down (Lawlor 1925; Bourke 2008), Armagh, Co. Armagh (Gailey & Harper 1984; Lynn 1977), 'New Graveyard', Clonmacnoise, Co. Offaly (Murphy 2003; T Young, pers. comm.), Ballyvourney, Co. Cork (O'Kelly 1952), Illaunloughan Island, Co. Kerry (White-Marshall & Walsh 2005), and Reask, Co. Kerry (Fanning 1981; Edwards 1990, 87). Recent excavations at secular enclosure sites have also produced large assemblages of iron-working waste, equivalent to the range of material discovered at Clonfad. At Johnstown 1, Co. Westmeath, 2 tonnes of iron-working residues were recovered (Clarke & Carlin 2008), while Lowpark, Co. Mayo, produced 1.3 tonnes (Wallace 2008; Gillespie 2008). The largest assemblage so far from a monastic site was 380 kg, recovered from the 'New Graveyard' excavations at Clonmacnoise, although several sites excavated in Dublin have yet to be fully analysed (T Young, pers. comm.).

Hand-bell manufacture

The archaeological evidence at Clonfad is dominated by large-scale and highly specialised iron-working during the early medieval period. Following his analysis, Dr Tim Young concluded that the most important activity carried out in the excavated portion of the monastery was the manufacture of iron hand-bells. This required advanced smithing technology for the complex and skilled production of the large iron sheets of a uniform thickness needed for the body of a hand-bell (Young, forthcoming). As a result, this was considered the pinnacle of the blacksmith's craft at this time, carried out without the aid of mechanised hammers or blast furnaces (Bourke 1980; 2008, 23).

The presence of fragments of the shroud, or clay coating, from the brazing process used to coat wrought-iron hand-bells (Illus. 7; Bourke 2008) is definitive evidence for production of Bourke's class 1 bell at the site, and 52 shroud fragments were found throughout the early medieval phases of the monastery. Class 1 hand-bells are more commonly found in Ireland than in Britain, with 50 examples from Ireland, 12 from Scotland, two from England and one from Wales (Illus. 8; Bourke 2008, 22). (Bourke's class 2 comprises cast-bronze hand-bells, which were not evidenced at Clonfad and are generally

Illus. 7—Brazing shroud fragments for hand-bell manufacture (Valerie J Keeley Ltd).

considered to be later in date.) Hand-bells have consequently been regarded as being a particular aspect of the Irish church, although Bourke (ibid.) has argued that they are not indigenous to Ireland and instead originate from Roman Britain and the Roman world more generally. The bells were imported from earlier devotional and domestic traditions, along with the chalice, paten and strainer, to become an essential part of the Christian liturgical equipment. The earliest historical reference to a hand-bell used in a monastic context is in a letter from Carthage (modern-day Tunisia) in AD 535 (ibid.). Within a century hand-bells had turned up in County Westmeath. Six examples of hand-bells are depicted on high crosses in Ireland between the eighth and 10th centuries. Production of the bells appears to have ceased by the 10th century, but individual examples were then enshrined as saints' reliquaries and in this way continued to be of significance (Bourke 1980, 59; 2008, 22–8).

The processes used to produce wrought-iron hand-bells are well documented elsewhere and the manufacturing process required what was cutting-edge technology at the time (Bourke 1980, 59; 2008). The process and techniques used to add the bronze coating to hand-bells were not previously known and these were tested by Dr Young through experimental reconstruction of two replica hand-bells (Illus. 9 & 10). The evidence recovered at Clonfad has proven to be most important both in identifying the technology used in the manufacturing process and in generating the earliest date so far recorded for the manufacture of this important piece of liturgical furniture in Europe (Bourke 2008, 22). (Dr Young has written an account of his experimental hand-bell reconstruction, which can be accessed at www.geoarch.co.uk/experimental/bell.html.)

Possible brazing shroud fragments have since been identified at Ballinglanna North, Co. Cork (J Tierney & T Young, pers. comm.), and it is likely that others will be identified at further sites in due course. Nevertheless, such additional material does not take from the

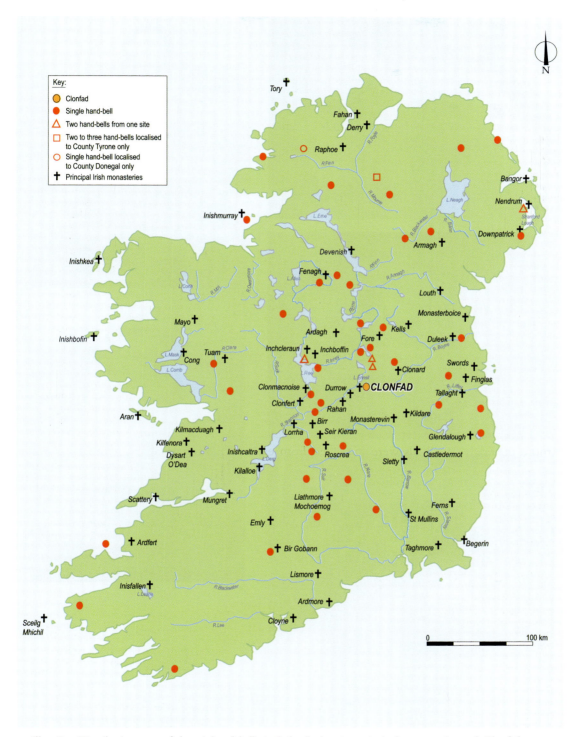

Illus. 8—Distribution map of class 1 hand-bells in Ireland, showing principal monasteries and Clonfad (after Bourke 1980; 2008).

Illus. 9—Part 1 of the experimental brazing process. (a) The two components of the wrought-iron bell are the main body (here cut out, ready to fold) and the handle/suspension loop (the handle is formed in this image, but the suspension loop is still straight to allow it to be passed through the hole in the bell body). (b) The finished forged bell. (c) The forged bell is wrapped in cloth, then the coil-built clay shroud is applied. The bronze in this experiment was placed around the lip of the bell, before the shroud was completed. (d) The brazing hearth, modelled on one of the excavated hearths. (e) The double-action bellows shown here are anachronistic; medieval smiths would probably have used a pair of single-action bellows (GeoArch Ltd).

Illus. 10—Part 2 of the experimental brazing process. (a) The brazing shroud exposed in the hearth at the end of the heating. In this case the shroud has a serious flaw (lower right) where the shroud has cracked. (b) The package is removed from the hearth and allowed to cool before being given a final quench to break it open. (c) The experimental clay shroud, showing the imprint of the end seam of the bell, with rivets, similar to the fragments in Illus. 7, and the remnants of the carbonised cloth. (d) The bell is dull when removed from the shroud because of oxide scale formation. (e) The bell is cleaned to remove the scale and the brazed surface is revealed (GeoArch Ltd).

fact that the Clonfad assemblage provides important new evidence for the use of brazing in the manufacturing process of iron hand-bells. It also demonstrates the importance attached to Clonfad as a central place of hand-bell manufacture. The extent of the metallurgical remains indicates mass production of hand-bells over several centuries rather than just a single bell. In the way that certain monasteries were known for their scriptoria and the manuscripts they produced, such as Iona in western Scotland, Clonfad must have been highly regarded for its manufacture of hand-bells.

Discussion

One of the most important discoveries made during the excavations at Clonfad has been the unique and important new evidence for the technologically advanced manufacture of wrought-iron hand-bells in the early medieval period. The Clonfad evidence suggests for the first time that a thin coat of bronze was applied by brazing.

The production and finishing of hand-bells at Clonfad has significant implications for the wider economic and organisational aspects of the early medieval period. A study of hand-bells has shown a distribution pattern that is focused on the Irish midlands, and extends to Scotland, Wales and England (Illus. 8; Bourke 1980; 2008). The production of hand-bells had a limited and exclusive patronage, as this type of bell was used exclusively by an abbot to call members of the monastic community to prayer and was a symbol of status and position. Furthermore, it required specialised expert smithing techniques, demanding considerable skill, knowledge, time and resources. It may be reasonable to assume that production centres were highly specialised and, if the record at Clonfad is any reflection, such centres focused on their product over a long period of time. Clonfad was well placed to serve in this capacity: it had ready access to the raw material; it was located in a political heartland close to the seat of power and wealth at Tara in the ancient kingdom of Mide; and it was ably positioned for access across the midlands by land (esker routeways) and by water.

Acknowledgements

Thanks to Rónán Swan and Orlaith Egan (NRA archaeologists), Peter Fegan (landowner), the excavation team, post-excavation and support staff of Valerie J Keeley Ltd (project managers), Dr Tim Young and Andrew Murphy (blacksmith at St Fagan's Folk Park). Thanks also to John Nicholls, Target Archaeological Geophysics, and Lisa Wilson (illustrations).

Note

1. NGR 240599, 240591; height 89–93 m OD; excavation reg. no. E2723; ministerial direction no. A003; Register of Historic Monuments 2009/01.

8. Charcoal production in medieval Ireland
Niall Kenny

The roots of charcoal production are likely to lie in the early prehistoric period, but it probably did not really intensify until the advent of metallurgy in the Bronze Age and the later development of iron technology. From late prehistory onwards, people in Ireland were actively engaged in the production of charcoal for industrial and domestic uses. Charcoal-making was an integral part of the iron-working process, without which the temperatures necessary for iron-smelting and smithing could not have been achieved (see Chapter 6). Charcoal would also have been important in the smelting and working of non-ferrous metals and, indeed, in other high-temperature crafts, such as glass- and enamel-working. The production of many high-status metal objects and weapons as well as more mundane everyday implements would simply not have been possible without it. Charcoal would also have been an important domestic fuel and was probably widely used for cooking in the past, as it was a 'clean' and virtually smokeless fuel.

Not much has been written about the charcoal production process in early medieval Ireland, however. Tylecote (1986, 225), referring not just to Ireland, noted that 'very little is known about the making of charcoal in the early periods'. Further to this, O'Sullivan & Harney (2007, 198) recently stated that 'charcoal producing pits are one of the most understudied areas in Irish early medieval archaeology'. This can largely be explained by the fact that there was, until relatively recently, little or no excavated archaeological evidence for charcoal production in early and late medieval Ireland. Furthermore, this situation was compounded by the almost complete lack of references to charcoal production in the early historical sources.

Recent development-led excavations, particularly on national road schemes, have dramatically changed the situation, and an abundance of evidence for charcoal production has now been uncovered. An extensive range of charcoal production pits have been excavated on NRA developments such as the M7 Portlaoise–Castletown/M8 Portlaoise–Cullahill motorway scheme, Co. Laois, the M4 Kinnegad–Enfield–Kilcock motorway scheme (M4 KEK) in counties Kildare, Meath and Westmeath, new sections of the N6 in counties Westmeath and Offaly between Kinnegad and Athlone, the N7 Nenagh–Limerick road scheme in counties Limerick and Tipperary, and the N21 Castleisland–Abbeyfeale road scheme in County Kerry. The majority of the dated pits were found to date from the early and late medieval periods.

Both charcoal production pits and charcoal production mounds (or platforms) have been recorded in Ireland. This paper outlines the importance of charcoal production in early and late medieval Ireland, focusing in particular on the large number of charcoal production pits excavated in recent years. The process of charcoal production and the various stages involved will be outlined with particular reference to ethnographic evidence. The overall aim of the paper is to highlight the important role played by the production and use of charcoal in the economy and the everyday lives of medieval people, the effort required to produce it, and the ingenuity and industrious nature of the people involved in its production.

Traditional methods of charcoal-making

Charcoal is produced when wood is burned under conditions where a restricted air supply prevents the complete combustion of the wood. In western countries such as Britain and Ireland, charcoal was produced in traditional earth kilns right up to the first half of the 20th century (Aaron 1980). There were two main types of traditional earth kilns: the pit kiln and the mound kiln (Illus. 1 & 2).

The early medieval law-tracts contain many references to metal-working and smithing (see Scott 1990, 171–212). Unfortunately, these early historical sources provide little or no insight into how, and in what circumstances, charcoal was produced in early medieval Ireland. The earliest historical account of a charcoal production feature is a classical description of a traditional mound kiln by the Greek philosopher Theophrastus in the fourth–third century BC. In his *Perí Fytón Historias* or *Historia Plantarum* Theophrastus describes how 'for charcoal burning they select smooth logs to be stacked densely in a pile; when they coat the pile with clay they ignite it and pierce holes in the coating' (cited in Pleiner 2000, 119). In his 16th-century AD treatise on metals and metallurgy the Italian Biringuccio documents the two traditional methods of charcoal production (Smith & Gnudi 1990, 173–9; Pleiner 2000, 119) (see Illus. 3). One method consisted of earth-dug

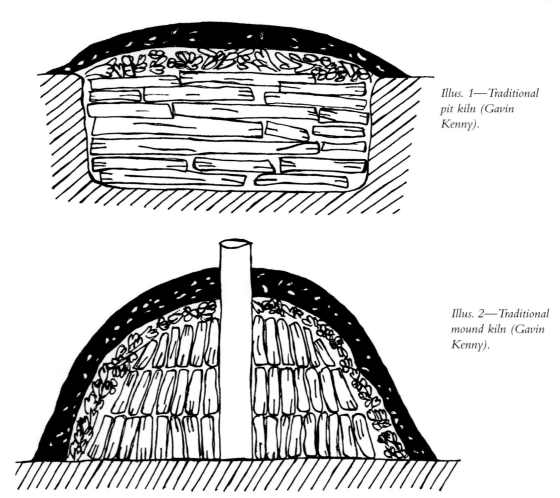

Illus. 1—Traditional pit kiln (Gavin Kenny).

Illus. 2—Traditional mound kiln (Gavin Kenny).

Illus. 3—A 16th-century depiction of the two main types of traditional earth kilns (mounds and pits) used for charcoal production (from Pleiner 2000, 120).

pits filled with wood, which were then set alight and covered with earth (traditional pit kilns). The other method consisted of clay- and vegetation-covered piles of stacked wood (traditional mound kilns). These two historical accounts from Europe, along with numerous other historical references from medieval England (see Armstrong 1979), illustrate the antiquity of charcoal production using both pit and mound kilns. Importantly, they also illustrate that these methods have essentially not changed for thousands of years. The two traditional methods of charcoal production are still in use in many developing countries today, such as Haiti, India, Malaysia and Thailand, and in many sub-Saharan African countries, for instance Uganda, Congo, Kenya and Zambia.

Traditional pit kilns
Pit kilns, or charcoal production pits, simply consisted of pits of varying shape and size cut into the ground. The pit was filled with fuel wood, which was usually carefully stacked (horizontally) to allow proper airflow throughout the kiln. Sometimes the wood would

have been stacked around a central post or stake, which was removed before firing to form a central chimney/firing space. The wood pile was then lit with charcoal and kindling, and when the wood was burning well the pit was completely covered and sealed with a layer of vegetation (normally leaves, bracken or grass turf) and subsequently with a layer of soil. (In the case of small pit kilns, a fire was usually made at the bottom of the kiln and wood was subsequently added to fill the pit, which was then sealed by a layer of vegetation and a layer of earth.) A number of holes were then punched into the outer covering in order to regulate the flow of air into the pit and thus control the carbonisation process.

The water contained in the wood is first evaporated by the heat of the fire, and when the temperature reaches over 270° C volatile gases and liquids (including tars and oils) are released from the wood (International Labour Office 1985, 50; Aaron 1980, 6). Once all the impurities and contaminants are expelled from the wood, the smoke becomes thin and turns from grey to blue or transparent. At this stage the carbonisation process is terminated as the wood has been turned into charcoal (International Labour Office 1985, 50). The already restricted airflow must be shut off (sealed with more soil) and the charcoal be allowed to cool down before it can safely be exposed to the open air for retrieval. During the process of carbonisation the volume of fuel wood is reduced, resulting in cracks appearing in the earthen seal covering the pit (ibid., 56). These cracks must be repaired immediately, otherwise the charcoal will completely combust, rendering the (labour-intensive) exercise unsuccessful.

The whole process could take about a week (depending on the size of the kiln and the amount of wood being carbonised), including the cooling-down period. During this time the charcoal-producers had to attend to and maintain the pit with vigour and patience. We can imagine that signs such as the shrinking of the pit content, the cracking of the earthen seal and the change in colour of the smoke would all have indicated to the charcoal-producers that the process of carbonisation was complete and so the airflow to the pit could then be cut off. Once the charcoal was extracted, the pit could be cleaned out for reuse. In some countries the traditional pit kiln was not used during wetter months or during rainy periods, as the intrusion of too much water into the pit would have spoiled the charcoal production process (ibid., 54).

Traditional mound kilns

Mound kilns, or charcoal production mounds, consisted of structured stacks of wood laid on the ground surface. Just like the pit kilns, they varied in shape and size. In rectangular mound kilns the wood was usually piled horizontally, whereas in circular and oval mound kilns the wood was usually stacked vertically in several layers around a central post or chimney (Illus. 4). The woodpile was then covered by a layer of vegetation and soil (Illus. 5) and the central post was removed. The kiln was fired by pouring hot charcoal and kindling down the central flue. Just like the pit kiln method, the carbonisation process was controlled by opening and closing air and smoke holes around the earthen covering (see Illus. 6 & 7). There is less labour involved in the construction and operation of mound kilns, and they tend to produce higher yields of charcoal (International Labour Office 1985, 56; Kimaryo & Ngereza 1989).

The charcoal production process was physically demanding and involved many laborious activities such as tree-felling, wood procurement and processing, as well as pit and mound construction and operation (see Table 1). The control and maintenance of the pits

Illus. 4—A traditional mound kiln from Wessex, England, 1939. Note the central pole around which the timber is stacked—this creates the central firing chimney once it is removed (from Armstrong 1979, 53).

Illus. 5—Vegetation- and soil-covered circular mound kiln from Bad Kohlgrub in southern Germany (Chris Adam).

Creative Minds

Illus. 6—Traditional mound kilns in operation near Pondicherry in south-east India (Chris Adam).

Illus. 7—Traditional mound kilns in south-east India. Note the woman attending to and repairing the outer earthen seal controlling the flow of air into the kiln (Chris Adam).

and mounds after firing required constant attention for long periods of time. The development of high temperatures in constricted and controlled environments was naturally a dangerous undertaking. A review of traditional charcoal production activities in Zambia highlighted various health risks associated with the process, including exposure to constant smoke and toxic gases, sore hands, backache and general exhaustion, as well as heat burns and chest pains (Hibajene & Kalumiana 1996).

Table 1—An outline of the main stages in the charcoal production process.

Stage	Relevant factors
1. Choice of location	Proximity to woodland resources, smelting and smithing sites, immediate topography
2. Procurement of wood	Woodland management (e.g. coppicing), procurement strategies (specific wood species), transport, seasoning/drying
3. Construction of kiln	Choice of kiln type (pit or mound), digging the pit/structuring and stacking of the wood, covering with vegetation and soil
4. Firing, maintenance and control	Controlling air flow/smoke outlet, repairing cracks/holes in the kiln covering, long, arduous process
5. Cooling and retrieval of charcoal	Allowing charcoal to cool fully, then harvesting and storing it in safe, dry conditions prior to cartage
6. Cleaning or abandonment of site	Clean the kiln for reuse or abandon site

The archaeological evidence for charcoal production in early and late medieval Ireland

The archaeological evidence seems to indicate the importance of the pit kiln method in medieval Ireland, with the discovery of hundreds of charcoal production pits on recent excavations. As noted earlier, both charcoal production pits and mounds have been recorded in Ireland. Charcoal production platforms (mounds) found in Glendalough, Co. Wicklow (Healy 1972), and elsewhere are described in a recent article by O'Sullivan & Downey (2009). Charcoal pits excavated in the course of recent development-led excavations are the main focus of this paper. Mound kilns may also have been in use in early medieval Ireland, but evidence of their existence and usage tends not to survive as well on development-led excavations because they would have been vulnerable to destruction by agricultural activities such as ploughing. Interestingly, a number of features on charcoal production sites at Kilcotton 1 and Kilcotton 2, Co. Laois[1] (Danaher et al. 2008a; 2008b), excavated on the M7/M8 motorway scheme, could represent the remains of traditional mound kilns. These features consisted of oval, circular and rectangular spreads with no definite cuts. They exhibited evidence for often intense *in situ* burning and were found to contain frequent to moderate charcoal inclusions. Numerous similar features have been identified on other charcoal production sites, and these need to be looked at in more detail in the future. It seems that the mound kiln became much more widely used in the late medieval and post-medieval periods in industrialised European countries for charcoal production associated with large-scale metal-working activities, e.g. at Cummeengeera, Co. Cork, Glendalough, Co. Wicklow (O'Sullivan & Downey 2009; Healy 1972), and around Sheffield, England (Ardron & Rotherham 1999).

The charcoal production pit in early and late medieval Ireland
The most common charcoal production kiln feature excavated on recent developments appears to be the charcoal production pit. These tend to consist of simple earth-cut, charcoal-filled pit features. They can be circular, oval or rectangular in shape and normally exhibit evidence for *in situ* burning on their base and sides. Usually there tends to be a charcoal-rich primary layer in the bottom of the pit, with upper secondary fills of soil also containing frequent charcoal inclusions. From the analysis of a corpus of 100 excavated charcoal production pits it appears that on average the rectangular/subrectangular pits were larger (2.42 m by 1.17 m by 0.24 m) than the circular (1.39 m by 1.22 m by 0.33 m) and oval (1.70 m by 1.13 m by 0.16 m) pits (Kenny 2008). Two of the 100 charcoal pits analysed were classified as irregularly shaped, 35 were rectangular/subrectangular, 35 circular and 28 oval. Examples of typical rectangular charcoal production pits include subrectangular pits excavated at Kilcotton 1 and Trumra 3, Co. Laois[2] (see Illus. 8) (O'Neill & Kane 2008), which measured 2.7 m by 1.3 m by 0.28 m and 2.4 m by 1.36 m by 0.28 m respectively. A number of larger rectangular pits have been excavated, including an example at Ballycorick, Co. Clare, which measured over 4 m in length (Grogan et al. 2007, 173), and two excavated at Kilmaniheen West, Co. Kerry,[3] which measured over 3 m in length (Hull & Taylor 2006). While there were some exceptions, it was generally found that the circular and oval pits tended to have concave/sloping sides, often leading to flat and sometimes even concave bases, while the rectangular examples were generally larger and had steeper, almost vertical, sides and flatter bases. A circular pit excavated at Russagh 4, Co. Offaly[4] (OCarroll 2009), which measured 1.16 m by 1.1 m by 0.13 m, is a typical example of a circular charcoal production pit (Illus. 9).

As a result of their larger size, rectangular charcoal production pits such as the one excavated at Kilbeggan South 3, Co. Westmeath[5] (Coughlan 2009a) (see Illus. 10), may have produced more charcoal than the smaller circular and oval pits. The rectangular examples tend to occur in association with iron-working sites much more frequently than the circular or oval examples, perhaps hinting at their more industrial nature. A number of excavated pits, most notably rectangular and subrectangular pits, were found to have their charcoal yields intact (i.e. the charcoal was not extracted from the pit after carbonisation). In some cases carbonised lengths of wood were recorded, aligned along the long axis of the pit kiln. The rectangular examples (e.g. Hardwood 3 and Newcastle 2, Co. Meath[6] (Murphy 2004; O'Hara 2003), and Trumra 3, Co. Laois) were often found to contain quite substantial unexploited charcoal yields. This is quite intriguing because, as outlined above, the charcoal production process was very labour-intensive, involving the investment of a lot of time and energy. It has been plausibly suggested by Carlin (2008, 101) that perhaps the charcoal pit became too wet, rendering the newly produced charcoal unsuitable to use, hence it was not harvested. It is also possible that a sudden event (such as warfare or a death, etc.) may have interrupted the extraction and use of the charcoal at these sites, or that certain cultural or social taboos prohibited its extraction and use. There are numerous possible explanations

Charcoal production in medieval Ireland

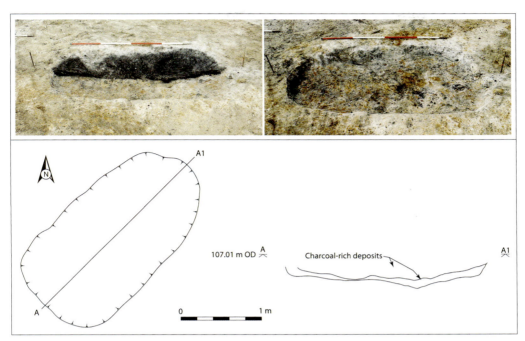

Illus. 8—Mid-excavation and post-excavation photos, plan and section drawing of a subrectangular charcoal production pit at Trumra 3, Co. Laois (Archaeological Consultancy Services Ltd).

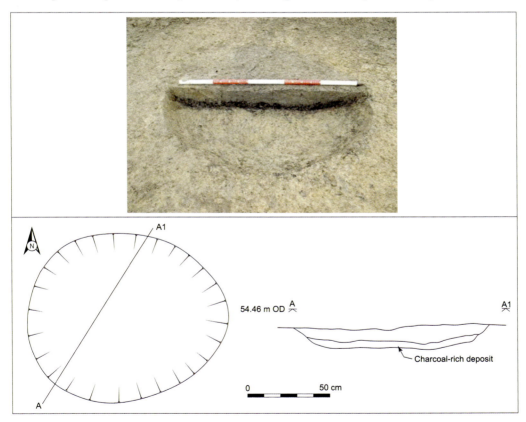

Illus. 9—Mid-excavation photo, plan and section of a circular charcoal production pit at Russagh 4, Co. Offaly (Irish Archaeological Consultancy Services Ltd).

Creative Minds

Illus. 10—Mid-excavation view of a rectangular charcoal production pit at Kilbeggan South 3, Co. Westmeath, facing south-west (Irish Archaeological Consultancy Services Ltd).

(economic, social and other) for why the charcoal was not extracted from some pits.

Specialist analysis on numerous sites established that many different wood species (such as oak, willow, alder, ash, elm and hazel) were being carbonised within the pits in the past. Oak appears to have been the dominant wood species used, however, and this was evident on numerous road schemes, such as the M4 KEK and M7/M8 motorway schemes and the N21 Castleisland–Abbeyfeale road scheme (Carlin 2008; OCarroll 2008; Hull & Taylor 2006). Hardwood charcoals such as oak, beech and birch do not crumble as easily as softwood charcoals during transport (Tylecote 1986, 225), and because of its high calorific values, longer burning time and higher temperature-producing properties oak is well suited for use in charcoal production associated with metal-working activities (OCarroll 2008). The presence or even predominance of one particular wood species (especially oak) within a pit is usually a good indicator that charcoal was being produced in it.

While hundreds of charcoal production pits have been identified on recent excavations, caution is necessary in interpreting every charcoal-rich pit or spread as a charcoal production site. Charcoal production must not become a convenient 'dumping ground' for all the unclassified miscellaneous charcoal features that turn up on excavations. It is therefore suggested that the following provisional criteria for identifying a charcoal production pit be adhered to until a more composite analysis of the charcoal production features is undertaken.

1. Charcoal production pits are by definition earth-cut pits—they must be definable cut features.
2. They usually exhibit evidence for *in situ* burning on their base and sides.
3. They usually have a charcoal-rich primary fill, with upper fills also containing frequent charcoal inclusions.
4. There is a notable absence of artefacts within the pits and on charcoal-making sites.
5. They can be (sub)circular, (sub)oval or (sub)rectangular in shape.
6. The rectangular examples tend to be larger and to have vertical or near-vertical sides and flat/gently sloping bases (although not always), while the circular and oval examples tend to have more concave sides leading to flat/sometimes concave bases (although not always).
7. If the pit is less than 0.7 m in diameter or length then its functionality as a charcoal production pit is questionable. Although small charcoal production pits are known, they tend to measure as follows: rectangular/subrectangular, 2.42 m by 1.17 m by 0.24 m; circular/subcircular, 1.39 m by 1.22 m by 0.33 m; oval/suboval, 1.7 m by 1.13 m by 0.16 m.
8. If only one wood species is present within the pit or dominates the assemblage (oak being the most common), this usually indicates that the pit primarily acted as a charcoal production pit.

The dating evidence

A list of 50 dated charcoal production features (mostly pits) was compiled from various published and unpublished sources (see Appendix 1). Illustrations 11–13 are calibration charts showing the span of these 50 features in chronological order from the Bronze Age to the late medieval period. The majority of the dated pits were found to fall within the early and late medieval periods, particularly the latter part of the early medieval period and the early part of the late medieval period (between the ninth and 13th centuries). Interestingly, many of the larger rectangular and subrectangular charcoal production pits were found to date from between the ninth and 13th centuries. Conversely, many circular and subcircular pits tend to date from the late medieval period (15th–17th centuries). Nevertheless, some circular/subcircular pits have been dated to the early medieval period and some rectangular pits to the late medieval period. Oval/suboval pits have also been dated to both the early and late medieval periods. This suggests that different types of charcoal production pits and different methods of charcoal production were being used at the same time in the past. Whether certain types of pits may have been more prevalent in certain areas, on particular sites or even in one particular period will need to be explored in more detail in the future.

The earliest dates returned came from two possible charcoal production pits excavated at Carrigatogher (site 2), Co. Tipperary[7] (MacLeod 2009), which were dated to the Bronze Age (1190–1002 BC, UBA-11800, and 1613–1500 BC, UBA-11803; see Appendix 1 for details). Another possible charcoal production pit excavated at Barnasallagh 1, Co. Laois[8] (Lennon 2008), returned an Iron Age date of 110 BC–AD 80 (SUERC-17973). Aside from these examples, very few charcoal production pits have been dated to the prehistoric or very early historic periods, but given that the roots of charcoal production most likely lie in the Bronze Age period, earlier dates for charcoal pits are expected in the future.

It appears that the charcoal production process altered little from the late prehistoric period until the late medieval period. This highlights the importance of scientific dating in furthering our knowledge of charcoal production in Ireland. The majority of the radiocarbon dates collated and presented in Illus. 11–13 and Appendix 1 were derived from oak charcoal samples and therefore we must consider the impact of the 'old wood effect' on our dating profile (Warner 1990). Oak trees can live up to 300–400 years and the dated samples could therefore be of a more recent date than the results indicate. If at all possible in the future, when charcoal samples are analysed from charcoal production pits, short-lived wood species (such as hazel) identified in the assemblage should be preferred for dating over oak. Nevertheless, the frustrating fact is that oak was the preferred wood species of the early wood collier, and oak and other long-lived wood species seem to dominate charcoal production assemblages. While we must be conscious of the impact of the old wood effect on our dating evidence, the results consistently point to an early and late medieval usage period (see Illus. 11–13 & Appendix 1).

Landscape context

Charcoal production pits were found to be predominantly located on gently sloping ground, often overlooking marshy or lower-lying wetter areas. Sloping ground would have drained more easily, allowing rain and surface water to run off, thus not interfering with the charcoal production process in the pit.

Charcoal production pits occur as single isolated pit features, in small clusters of two to four pits, in large clusters of scattered pits, and on small- or large-scale single- and multiperiod iron-working sites. A number of charcoal production pits were excavated on an early to late medieval iron-working site at Aghamore, Co. Westmeath (Grogan et al. 2007, 333–4). Several possible charcoal production pits were also excavated on an Iron Age iron-working site at Derrinsallagh 4, Co. Laois[9] (Lennon & Kane 2009). On the M4 KEK excavations a number of charcoal production pits were excavated on single- and multiperiod iron-working sites (Carlin 2008). Large clusters of charcoal production pits were excavated on sites such as Kilcotton 1 (49 pits) and Kilcotton 2 (17 pits), Co. Laois, on the M7/M8, and Kilmaniheen West, Co. Kerry (16 pits), on the N21 (Hull & Taylor 2006). In the case of Kilcotton 1 and 2 the radiocarbon dating evidence seems to indicate that they were revisited and reused at different stages in the early and late medieval periods and not just on one occasion.

Kilcotton 1 and 2, along with most other charcoal production sites, were probably situated close to abundant and suitable woodland resources away from the main areas of

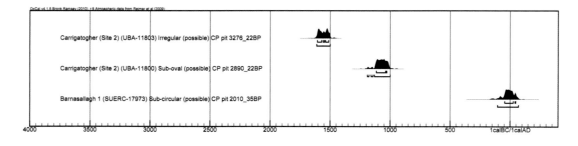

Illus. 11—Chart showing the calibration of radiocarbon dates from prehistoric and early historic charcoal production pits/features.

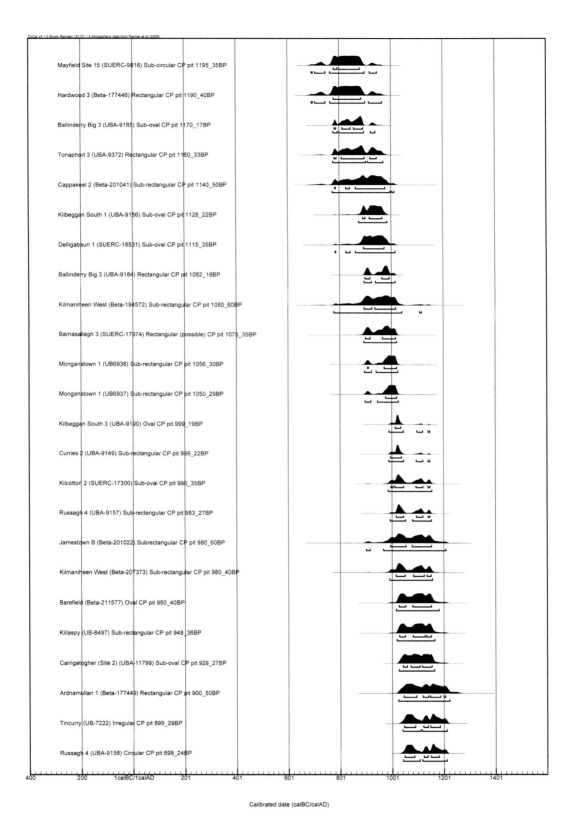

Illus. 12—Chart showing the calibration of radiocarbon dates from early medieval charcoal production pits/features.

Creative Minds

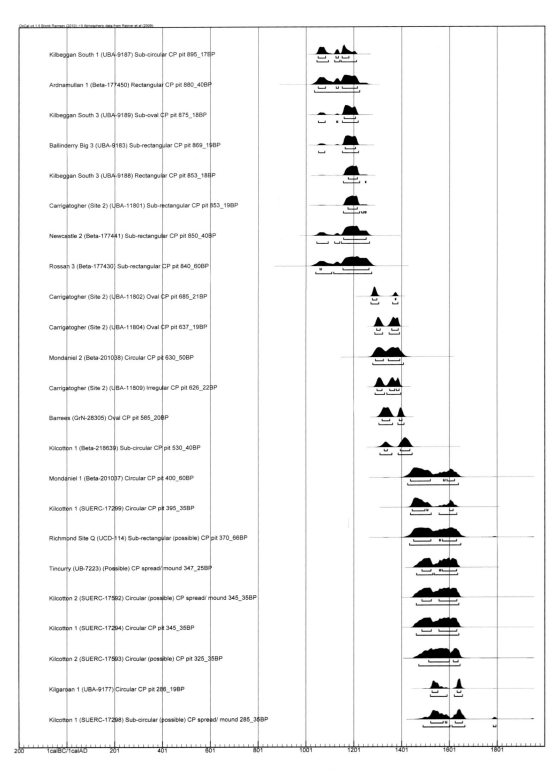

Illus. 13—Chart showing the calibration of radiocarbon dates from early and late medieval charcoal production pits/features.

settlement. It is possible that temporary dwellings may have been built on some of the larger charcoal production sites for the duration of the charcoal-making process, but evidence of this in the archaeological record needs to be looked at in more detail. It also appears that the charcoal production sites at Kilcotton and several smaller charcoal-making sites in the vicinity were located quite close to a number of contemporary iron-working sites. In fact, the entire landscape along this particular stretch of the M7/M8 appears to have been a haven for charcoal production and iron-working activities from the Iron Age period, through early medieval times and right up until the late medieval period.

Impact on the landscape

Charcoal production has had and continues to have a dramatic impact on many landscapes across the world today. As early as the 13th century measures were being introduced in southern England to control woodland clearance associated with charcoal production (Armstrong 1979; Schubert 1957; Hart 1968). Charcoal production activities at some of the larger-scale and longer-term charcoal-making sites may have involved the felling of considerable areas of woodland, almost certainly significantly altering the physical landscape. In saying that, analysis of the charcoal remains from numerous charcoal production sites on the M7/M8 indicated that wood colliers may have been using fast-growing coppiced oak and hazel from managed woodlands in the locality (OCarroll 2008). This suggests that some degree of woodland management and coppicing strategies may have been employed in the past to control the impact of charcoal production on local woodland resources—particularly oak supplies.

Palaeoenvironmental research carried out in association with excavations and specialist charcoal analysis on a number of metal-working sites in north-west Wales (at Bryn y Castell and Llwyn Du in Snowdonia) indicated that the impact of charcoal production and metal-working activities on the surrounding vegetation varied. At Bryn y Castell the impact upon the woodlands was apparent although not drastic, while at Llwyn Du it was clear that the surrounding woodland was being carefully managed in order to provide a sustainable fuel supply (Crew & Mighall, forthcoming; Mighall & Chambers 1997; Mighall et al. 2006). Similar scientific studies are much needed in Ireland and one such study is currently being undertaken by Ellen OCarroll (see Chapter 4).

Who were the charcoal-producers in early medieval times?

The production of charcoal by traditional methods does not involve the use of any specialised tools and therefore it could be (and still can be) undertaken by local communities, and essentially by any farmer with access to wood resources. It is generally accepted that in early medieval times small-scale iron-working activities were being undertaken by farmers and less-skilled members of society at their own occupation sites (Edwards 1990, 86). It is likely, then, that early medieval farmers also produced their own charcoal for small-scale metal-working and for use in the domestic household. This may account for many of the isolated charcoal production pits and clusters of pits that have been excavated throughout Ireland in recent years. The eighth-century law-tract *Críth Gablach* lists among the household possessions for one grade of farmer (the *mruigfher*) 'a sack of charcoal for irons' (Scott 1990, 100), suggesting that households may have had their own store of charcoal for the production of iron. Furthermore, charcoal was also seemingly produced by the early iron-workers on iron-working sites such as Aghamore, Co. Westmeath, Derrinsallagh 4, Co. Laois, and on numerous other iron-working sites excavated on the M4 KEK. Full-time or professional colliers may also have been engaged in the past in meeting the demands of larger secular metal-working sites, and indeed the demands and needs of ecclesiastical settlements and metal-working sites.

Conclusions

We are only starting to come to terms with the abundance of evidence for charcoal production in early and late medieval Ireland, and much more work remains to be carried out. There is a need for palaeoenvironmental research of the landscapes where charcoal production activities were taking place, and ideally this should be conducted in association with specialist analysis of the charcoal remains. More in-depth ethnographical studies and experimental archaeology (visit http://irishcharcoal.weebly.com/ for information on recent experiments) are also required in order to investigate the social aspects of charcoal-making as well as the more detailed practical workings of charcoal production kilns.

Nonetheless, it is becoming increasingly clear, much more so than ever before, that charcoal-making was an ancient and widespread tradition in Ireland and that the production and use of charcoal played an important part in the economy and everyday lives of medieval people. It is evident that the charcoal production pit, a prominent feature on many recent excavations, was very important in early and late medieval Ireland. It seems likely, however, that mound kilns may also have been in use in the early medieval period. It is apparent that charcoal pits continued to be used alongside charcoal production mounds in the late medieval period but that mound kilns became more common in the post-medieval period in association with the larger-scale industrial ironworks of the 17th century.

The large number of charcoal production kilns excavated in recent years are important testaments to the past activities associated with the charcoal production process—activities such as tree-felling and wood procurement, woodland management and coppicing, kiln construction and operation. Even more significantly, however, they are important testaments to the industrious and hard-working nature of the people involved in the production of charcoal in early and late medieval Ireland.

Acknowledgements

I would like to thank Jonathan Kinsella, Professor Liam Downey and Brian Dolan for commenting on early drafts of the paper. Many thanks to Deirdre Murphy (Archaeological Consultancy Services Ltd), Fintan Walsh (Irish Archaeological Consultancy Ltd), Graham Hull (TVAS [Ireland] Ltd), Patricia Long (Headland Archaeology Ltd), Bernice Molloy (Margaret Gowen & Co. Ltd) and John Tierney (Eachtra Archaeological Projects) for kindly supplying unpublished excavation reports and radiocarbon dating information relating to the many charcoal production sites excavated by their companies in recent years. I am very grateful to Professor William O'Brien and Dr Michelle Comber for providing me with details on the charcoal pit excavated at Barrees, Co. Cork. Thanks to Chris Adam, Tim Coughlan, Deirdre Murphy, Ellen OCarroll and Fintan Walsh for permission to reproduce their photographs and drawings. Special thanks to Martin Halpin (ACS Ltd) for his work on the excavation illustrations and to Gavin Kenny for producing the fine diagrams of the pit and mound kilns. Finally, thanks to the archaeologists and excavation directors who so diligently and professionally excavated and recorded the sites.

This paper is dedicated to the memory of Dr Blaze O'Connor, who will be sadly missed by her former students and will be remembered always as a wonderful archaeologist and a fantastic teacher.

Notes

1. Kilcotton 1: NGR 230117, 185382; height 120 m OD; excavation reg. no. E2187; ministerial direction no. A015; excavation director Ed Danaher. Kilcotton 2: NGR 230333, 185332; height 120 m OD; excavation reg. no. E2188; ministerial direction no. A015; excavation director Ed Danaher.
2. Trumra 3: NGR 239892, 193997; height 100 m OD; excavation reg. no. E2280; ministerial direction no. A015; excavation director Tara O'Neill.
3. Kilmaniheen West: NGR 109440, 123180; height 75.5 m OD; excavation licence no. 04E0975; excavation director Kate Taylor.
4. Russagh 4: NGR 225863, 237891; height 55 m OD; excavation reg. no. E2681; ministerial direction no. A016; excavation director Ellen OCarroll.
5. Kilbeggan South 3: NGR 233510, 234344; height 67 m OD; excavation reg. no. E3283; ministerial direction no. A016; excavation director Tim Coughlan.
6. Hardwood 3: NGR 260769, 244641; height 76 m OD; excavation licence no. 02E1141; excavation director Deirdre Murphy. Newcastle 2: NGR 276493, 240661; height 74 m OD; excavation licence no. 02E1093; excavation director Robert O'Hara.
7. Carrigatogher (site 2): NGR 181815, 176827; height 78.28 m OD; excavation reg. no. E2407; ministerial direction no. A026; excavation director Ross MacLeod.
8. Barnasallagh 1: NGR 227431, 186262; height 120 m OD; excavation reg. no. E2205; ministerial direction no. A015; excavation director Anne-Marie Lennon.
9. Derrinsallagh 4: NGR 225065, 185647; height 121.09 m OD; excavation reg. no. E2180; ministerial direction no. A015; excavation director Anne-Marie Lennon.

Appendix 1—Radiocarbon dates from excavated archaeological sites described in these proceedings

Notes

1. Radiocarbon ages are quoted in conventional years BP (before AD 1950), and the errors for these dates are expressed at the one-sigma (68% probability) level of confidence.

2. Calibrated date ranges are equivalent to the probable calendrical age of the sample material and are expressed at one-sigma (68% probability) and two-sigma (95% probability) levels of confidence.

3. Dates obtained from Beta Analytic in Florida (Beta lab code) were calibrated using either the IntCal98 (Stuiver et al. 1998) or IntCal04 (Reimer et al. 2004) calibration data sets and the Talma & Vogel 1993 calibration programme in the case of sites referred to in Chapter 6, and using IntCal98 and the OxCal v.3.10 calibration programme (Bronk Ramsey 2005) in the case of sites referred to in Chapter 8.

Dates obtained from the University of Groningen, Netherlands (GrN and GrA lab codes), were calibrated using data sets from Stuiver & Reimer 1993 and IntCal04 and the CALIB 5.0.2. calibration programme (Stuiver et al. 2005) in the case of sites referred to in Chapters 6, 7 and 8.

Dates obtained from Queen's University, Belfast (UB and UBA lab codes), were calibrated using data sets from Stuiver & Reimer 1993 and IntCal04 and the CALIB 5.0.2 calibration programme in the case of sites referred to in Chapters 1, 6, 7 and 8.

Dates obtained from the Scottish Universities Environmental Research Centre (SUERC lab code) were calibrated using either IntCal98 or IntCal04 and OxCal v.3.10 in the case of sites referred to in Chapter 8.

The date obtained from University College Dublin (UCD lab code) cited in Chapter 8 was calibrated using IntCal98 and CALIB 5.0.2.

Dates obtained from Waikato Laboratory, New Zealand (Wk lab code), were calibrated using IntCal98 and OxCal v.3.10 in the case of Chapter 5.

Dates from Barrees, Co. Cork (GrN-28305), Monganstown 1, Co. Westmeath (UB-6937 & UB-6938), and Tincurry, Co. Tipperary (UB-7222 & UB-7223), cited in Chapter 8, were calibrated using IntCal04 and the OxCal v.4.1 calibration programme (Bronk Ramsey 2009).

Lab code	Site	Sample/context	Yrs BP	Calibrated date ranges

Ch. 1 (F Sternke)—From boy to man: 'rights' of passage and the lithic assemblage from a Neolithic mound in Tullahedy, Co. Tipperary

Lab code	Site	Sample/context	Yrs BP	Calibrated date ranges
UBA-11160	Tullahedy	Wheat (*Triticum* spp) grains from uppermost fill of palisade foundation trench	4783 ± 32	3637–3628 BC one sigma 3644–3518 BC two sigma
UBA-11161	Tullahedy	Hazelnut (*Corylus avellana* L.) shell from basal fill of palisade foundation trench	4789 ± 24	3637–3630 BC one sigma 3641–3623 BC two sigma
UBA-11163	Tullahedy	Hazelnut (*Corylus avellana* L.) shell from post-occupation layer sealing structures 1 and 2	4776 ± 30	3635–3627 BC one sigma 3641–3518 BC two sigma
UBA-11166	Tullahedy	Charred seed or hazelnut shell from a layer immediately below the infill layers on the south-eastern side of the mound	4840 ± 26	3654–3634 BC one sigma 3694–3680 BC two sigma
UBA-11169	Tullahedy	Wheat (*Triticum* spp) grains from basal fill of hearth between structures 1 and 2	4770 ± 25	3634–3627 BC one sigma 3638–3520 BC two sigma
UBA-11173	Tullahedy	Wheat (*Triticum* spp) grains from cut of structure 2 foundation trench	4738 ± 24	3631–3578 BC one sigma 3633–3554 BC two sigma
UBA-11175	Tullahedy	Wheat (*Triticum* spp) grains from a charcoal-rich spread sealing pits associated with structure 2	4856 ± 25	3659–3637 BC one sigma 3696–3634 BC two sigma
UBA-11177	Tullahedy	Wheat (*Triticum* spp) grains from post-occupation layer sealing structure 1	4876 ± 24	3693–3682 BC one sigma 3699–3639 BC two sigma
UBA-11178	Tullahedy	Wheat (*Triticum* spp) grains from a charcoal-rich fill of structure 1 foundation trench	4756 ± 34	3633–3618 BC one sigma 3638–3508 BC two sigma
UBA-11179	Tullahedy	Charred seed or hazelnut shell from the cut of a post-hole in structure 3	4826 ± 24	3648–3633 BC one sigma 3655–3629 BC two sigma

Appendix 1

Lab code	Site	Sample/context	Yrs BP	Calibrated date ranges
UBA-11182	Tullahedy	Hazelnut (*Corylus avellana* L.) shell from basal fill of pit within structure 2	4718 ± 33	3627–3591 BC one sigma 3632–3558 BC two sigma

Ch. 5 (C Moore & C Chiriotti)—Reinventing the wheel: new evidence from Edercloon, Co. Longford

Lab code	Site	Sample/context	Yrs BP	Calibrated date ranges
Wk-20961	EDC 5	Birch (*Betula*) brushwood from base of togher directly over the block wheel	2909 ± 39	1190–1020 BC one sigma 1206–970 BC two sigma
Wk-25202	EDC 12/13	Ash (*Fraxinus*) brushwood from the base of the trackway	3034 ± 30	1380–1260 BC one sigma 1410–1210 BC two sigma
Wk-25203	EDC 49	Hazel (*Corylus*) brushwood from the base of the trackway	1241 ± 36	AD 680–860 one sigma AD 680–880 two sigma
Wk-25204	EDC 12/13	Hazel (*Corylus*) brushwood adjacent to the wheel rim	2397 ± 39	520–400 BC one sigma 750–390 BC two sigma

Ch. 6 (A Wallace & L Anguilano)—Iron-smelting and smithing: new evidence emerging on Irish road schemes

Lab code	Site	Sample/context	Yrs BP	Calibrated date ranges
Beta-171418	Curraheen 1	Ash (*Fraxinus*) charcoal from fill of pit	2210 ± 60	375–185 BC one sigma 395–100 BC two sigma
Beta-177427	Kinnegad 2	Oak (*Quercus* spp) charcoal from possible domestic hearth	2530 ± 60	790–540 BC one sigma 810–420 BC two sigma
Beta-177428	Kinnegad 2	Ash (*Fraxinus excelsior*) charcoal from bowl furnace	2270 ± 40	390–240 BC one sigma 400–210 BC two sigma
Beta-177434	Rossan 6	Oak (*Quercus*) charcoal from primary fill of charcoal platform	2610 ± 40	810–790 BC one sigma 820–780 BC two sigma
Beta-177435	Rossan 6	Oak (*Quercus*) charcoal from fill of bowl furnace	2150 ± 50	350–110 BC one sigma 370–50 BC two sigma
Beta-177442	Johnstown 3	Oak (*Quercus*) charcoal from fill of bowl furnace	2320 ± 50	400–380 BC one sigma 420–230 BC two sigma
Beta-201099	Lisnagar Demesne 1	Oak (*Quercus*) charcoal from furnace deposit	2180 ± 60	360–170 BC one sigma 390–50 BC two sigma

Lab code	Site	Sample/context	Yrs BP	Calibrated date ranges
Beta-231648	Lowpark	Oak (*Quercus*) charcoal from pit in iron-working area 1	1270 ± 40	AD 680–780 one sigma AD 660–870 two sigma
Beta-231651	Lowpark	Young oak (*Quercus*) charcoal from pit in iron-working area 2	1180 ± 40	AD 780–890 one sigma AD 720–970 two sigma
Beta-231653	Lowpark	Oak (*Quercus*) charcoal from pit in iron-working area 3	1320 ± 40	AD 660–690 one sigma AD 650–770 two sigma
Beta-231662	Lowpark	Oak (*Quercus*) charcoal from pit in iron-working area 4	1430 ± 40	AD 600–650 one sigma AD 560–660 two sigma
GrN-29489	Transtown AR29	Oak (*Quercus*) charcoal from charcoal-rich spread of furnace	2220 ± 40	364–208 BC one sigma 387–197 BC two sigma
UB-6316	Newrath, site 35	Hazel (*Corylus avellana*) charcoal from fill of burnt pit	2125 ± 33	196–110 BC one sigma 351–94 BC two sigma
UB-6317	Newrath, site 35	Oak (*Quercus* sp.) charcoal from fill of pit	2259 ± 33	391–261 BC one sigma 397–207 BC two sigma
UB-6763	Tonybaun	Ash (*Fraxinus*) and willow (*Ilex*) charcoal from possible smithing hearth	2045 ± 33	98 BC–AD 1 one sigma 166 BC–AD 25 two sigma
UB-6765	Tonybaun	Oak (*Quercus*) charcoal from fill of stone-lined furnace	2309 ± 35	405–363 BC one sigma 477–210 BC two sigma
UBA-12501	Borris, site AR33	Oak (*Quercus* sp.) charcoal from uppermost fill of pit	1272 ± 18	AD 688–770 one sigma AD 680–774 two sigma

Ch. 7 (P Stevens)—For whom the bell tolls: the monastic site at Clonfad 3, Co. Westmeath

Lab code	Site	Sample/context	Yrs BP	Calibrated date ranges
GrA-33802	Clonfad 3	Animal bone from brazing hearth	1335 ± 35	AD 651–762 one sigma AD 656–732 two sigma
GrA-33803	Clonfad 3	Animal bone from floor of smithy	1165 ± 35	AD 781–939 one sigma AD 803–925 two sigma
GrA-33804	Clonfad 3	Animal bone from floor of smithy	1215 ± 35	AD 772–878 one sigma AD 734–856 two sigma
UBA-8116	Clonfad 3	Charred cereal grains (hulled barley, barley, free-threshing wheat) and seeds and grasses (cabbage, pea, woodruff/bedstraw) from stone-lined cereal-drying kiln C147	166 ± 38	AD 1666–1952 one sigma AD 1660–1953 two sigma

Appendix 1

Lab code	Site	Sample/context	Yrs BP	Calibrated date ranges
UBA-8117	Clonfad 3	Charred cereal grains (hulled barley, two-row barley, rye, wheat and oat) and seeds and grasses (orache, waterpepper, small waterpepper, black bindweed, knotweeds, sheep's sorrel, curled dock, wild turnip, garden pea, hempnettle, bellflower, woodruff, stinking chamomile, corn marigold) from stone-lined cereal-drying kiln C217	751 ± 39	AD 1228–1283 one sigma AD 1211–1376 two sigma
UBA-8118	Clonfad 3	Charred cereal grains (hulled barley, barley, free-threshing wheat) and seeds (cabbage, pea, woodruff/bedstraw) from stone-lined cereal-drying kiln C147	203 ± 24	AD 1659–1951 one sigma AD 1650–1951 two sigma
UBA-8119	Clonfad 3	Charred cereal grains (hulled barley, barley, free-threshing wheat) and seeds and grasses (cabbage, pea, woodruff/bedstraw) from stone-lined cereal-drying kiln C147	120 ± 28	AD 1686–1927 one sigma AD 1680–1953 two sigma
UBA-8120	Clonfad 3	Charred grain (hulled barley, rye, oat and free-threshing wheat) and seeds and grasses (orache, common chickweed, lesser stitchwort, sedges, curled dock, wild turnip, lentil, garden pea; weeds: ribwort plantain, woodruff, hawk's beard, stinking chamomile, reed) from basal layer of stone-lined cereal-drying kiln C411	117 ± 25	AD 1689–1925 one sigma AD 1681–1953 two sigma

Lab code	Site	Sample/context	Yrs BP	Calibrated date ranges
UBA-8121	Clonfad 3	Charred grain (hulled barley grain) and seeds (woodruff and brome) from mid-level peat layer of stone-lined cereal-drying kiln C411	154 ± 22	AD 1674–1941 one sigma AD 1667–1953 two sigma
UBA-8216	Clonfad 3	Apple-type (Pomoideae) charcoal from mid-level infill of outer enclosing ditch	1199 ± 30	AD 779–874 one sigma AD 713–937 two sigma
UBA-8217	Clonfad 3	Oak (*Quercus*) charcoal from mid-level infill of outer enclosing ditch	1224 ± 33	AD 722–868 one sigma AD 689–886 two sigma
UBA-8218	Clonfad 3	Oak (*Quercus*) charcoal from lower-level infill of outer enclosing ditch	1281 ± 30	AD 680–770 one sigma AD 662–800 two sigma
UBA-8219	Clonfad 3	Hazel (*Corylus*) and alder (*Alnus*) charcoal from lower-level infill of outer enclosing ditch	1231 ± 31	AD 713–863 one sigma AD 688–882 two sigma
UBA-8220	Clonfad 3	Oak (*Quercus*) charcoal from stone-lined pit/trough	1206 ± 33	AD 778–867 one sigma AD 723–889 two sigma
UBA-8221	Clonfad 3	Oak (*Quercus*) charcoal from floor of smithy	1187 ± 23	AD 782–883 one sigma AD 774–933 two sigma
UBA-8679	Clonfad 3	Oak (*Quercus*) charcoal from inner enclosing ditch	1235 ± 31	AD 694–860 one sigma AD 688–878 two sigma
UBA-8680	Clonfad 3	Oak (*Quercus*) charcoal from linear ditch	1579 ± 20	AD 433–534 one sigma AD 427–538 two sigma

Ch. 8 (N Kenny)—Charcoal production in medieval Ireland

Lab code	Site	Sample/context	Yrs BP	Calibrated date ranges
Beta-177450	Ardnamullan 1, Co. Meath	Oak (*Quercus*) charcoal from primary fill of rectangular charcoal production pit	880 ± 40	AD 1060–1210 one sigma AD 1030–1250 two sigma
Beta-177449	Ardnamullan 1, Co. Meath	Oak (*Quercus*) and willow (*Salix*) charcoal from secondary fill of rectangular charcoal production pit	900 ± 50	AD 1040–1200 one sigma AD 1020–1250 two sigma

Appendix 1

Lab code	Site	Sample/context	Yrs BP	Calibrated date ranges
UBA-9184	Ballinderry Big 3, Co. Westmeath	Oak (*Quercus*) charcoal from primary fill of rectangular charcoal production pit	1082 ± 18	AD 899–922 one sigma AD 896–1014 two sigma
UBA-9185	Ballinderry Big 3, Co. Westmeath	Short-lived oak (*Quercus*) charcoal from primary fill of suboval charcoal production pit	1170 ± 17	AD 783–892 one sigma AD 779–940 two sigma
UBA-9183	Ballinderry Big 3, Co. Westmeath	Short-lived oak (*Quercus*) charcoal from primary fill of subrectangular charcoal production pit	869 ± 19	AD 1164–1208 one sigma AD 1054–1219 two sigma
Beta-211577	Barefield, Co. Clare	Elm (*Ulmus*) charcoal from fill of oval charcoal production pit	950 ± 40	AD 1020–1160 one sigma AD 1010–1180 two sigma
SUERC-17973	Barnasallagh 1, Co. Laois	Hazel (*Corylus avellana*) charcoal from primary fill of possible subcircular charcoal production pit	2010 ± 35	50 BC–AD 50 one sigma 110 BC–AD 80 two sigma
SUERC-17974	Barnasallagh 3, Co. Laois	Oak (*Quercus*) charcoal from primary fill of possible rectangular charcoal production pit	1075 ± 35	AD 890–1020 one sigma AD 890–1020 two sigma
GrN-28305	Barrees, Co. Cork	Oak (*Quercus*) charcoal from basal layer of oval charcoal production pit	585 ± 20	AD 1319–1402 one sigma AD 1306–1411 two sigma
Beta-201041	Cappakeel 2, Co. Laois	Oak (*Quercus*) charcoal from subrectangular charcoal production pit	1140 ± 50	AD 870–980 one sigma AD 780–1000 two sigma
UBA-11799	Carrigatogher (site 2), Co. Tipperary	Alder (*Alnus*) charcoal from primary deposit of suboval charcoal production pit	929 ± 27	AD 1042–1154 one sigma AD 1028–1164 two sigma
UBA-11800	Carrigatogher (site 2), Co. Tipperary	Hazel (*Corylus avellana*) charcoal from primary fill of possible suboval charcoal production pit	2890 ± 22	1116–1029 BC one sigma 1190–1002 BC two sigma
UBA-11801	Carrigatogher (site 2), Co. Tipperary	Hazel (*Corylus avellana*) charcoal from the primary fill of subrectangular pit	853 ± 19	AD 1177–1215 one sigma AD 1157–1251 two sigma

Lab code	Site	Sample/context	Yrs BP	Calibrated date ranges
UBA-11802	Carrigatogher (site 2), Co. Tipperary	Oak (*Quercus*) charcoal from upper fill of oval charcoal production pit	685 ± 21	AD 1279–1376 one sigma AD 1274–1385 two sigma
UBA-11803	Carrigatogher (site 2), Co. Tipperary	Charred hazelnut shell (*Corylus*) from the primary fill of possible irregular charcoal production pit	3276 ± 22	1607–1514 BC one sigma 1613–1500 BC two sigma
UBA-11804	Carrigatogher (site 2), Co. Tipperary	Hazel (*Corylus avellana*) charcoal from primary fill of oval charcoal production pit	637 ± 19	AD 1296–1387 one sigma AD 1289–1392 two sigma
UBA-11809	Carrigatogher (site 2), Co. Tipperary	Pomoideae charcoal from primary charcoal layer of irregular charcoal production pit	626 ± 22	AD 1298–1390 one sigma AD 1291–1396 two sigma
UBA-9149	Curries 2, Co. Westmeath	Alder (*Alnus* sp.) charcoal from basal fill of subrectangular charcoal production pit	999 ± 22	AD 997–1037 one sigma AD 989–1148 two sigma
SUERC-18531	Delligabaun 1, Co. Laois	Pomoideae charcoal from primary fill of suboval charcoal production pit	1115 ± 35	AD 890–975 one sigma AD 860–1020 two sigma
Beta-177446	Hardwood 3, Co. Meath	Alder (*Alnus glutinosa*) charcoal from rectangular charcoal production pit	1190 ± 40	AD 780–890 one sigma AD 720–960 two sigma
Beta-201022	Jamestown B, Co. Laois	Oak (*Quercus*) charcoal from primary fill of subrectangular charcoal production pit	980 ± 60	AD 1000–1150 one sigma AD 970–1190 two sigma
UBA-9186	Kilbeggan South 1, Co. Westmeath	Young oak (*Quercus*) charcoal from primary fill of suboval charcoal production pit	1128 ± 22	AD 891–966 one sigma AD 877–984 two sigma
UBA-9187	Kilbeggan South 1, Co. Westmeath	Oak (*Quercus*) charcoal from primary fill of subcircular charcoal production pit	895 ± 17	AD 1051–1178 one sigma AD 1045–1211 two sigma
UBA-9188	Kilbeggan South 3, Co. Westmeath	Elm (*Ulmus*) charcoal from primary fill of rectangular charcoal production pit	853 ± 18	AD 1178–1215 one sigma AD 1157–1251 two sigma
UBA-9189	Kilbeggan South 3, Co. Westmeath	Young oak (*Quercus*) charcoal from suboval charcoal production pit	875 ± 18	AD 1160–1207 one sigma AD 1052–1217 two sigma

Appendix 1

Lab code	Site	Sample/context	Yrs BP	Calibrated date ranges
UBA-9190	Kilbeggan South 3, Co. Westmeath	Young oak (*Quercus*) charcoal from primary fill of oval charcoal production pit	999 ± 19	AD 1014–1035 one sigma AD 990–1146 two sigma
SUERC-17294	Kilcotton 1, Co. Laois	Oak (*Quercus*) charcoal from primary fill of circular charcoal production pit	345 ± 35	AD 1480–1640 one sigma AD 1460–1640 two sigma
SUERC-17298	Kilcotton 1, Co. Laois	Oak (*Quercus*) charcoal from primary fill of possible subcircular charcoal production mound (spread)	285 ± 35	AD 1520–1660 one sigma AD 1490–1670 two sigma
SUERC-17299	Kilcotton 1, Co. Laois	Oak (*Quercus*) charcoal from primary charcoal layer of circular charcoal production pit	395 ± 35	AD 1440–1620 one sigma AD 1430–1640 two sigma
Beta-218639	Kilcotton 1, Co. Laois	Oak (*Quercus*) charcoal from primary charcoal layer of subcircular charcoal production pit	530 ± 40	AD 1400–1430 one sigma AD 1320–1440 two sigma
SUERC-17300	Kilcotton 2, Co. Laois	Oak (*Quercus*) charcoal from primary fill of suboval charcoal production pit	990 ± 35	AD 990–1150 one sigma AD 980–1160 two sigma
SUERC-17592	Kilcotton 2, Co. Laois	Oak (*Quercus*) charcoal from primary fill of possible circular charcoal production mound (charcoal spread)	345 ± 35	AD 1480–1640 one sigma AD 1460–1640 two sigma
SUERC-17593	Kilcotton 2, Co. Laois	Willow (*Salix*) charcoal from primary fill of possible circular charcoal production pit	325 ± 35	AD 1510–1640 one sigma AD 1470–1650 two sigma
UBA-9177	Kilgaroan 1, Co. Westmeath	Oak (*Quercus*) charcoal from primary fill of circular charcoal production pit	286 ± 19	AD 1528–1648 one sigma AD 1521–1656 two sigma
UB-6497	Killaspy 14, Co. Kilkenny	Oak (*Quercus*) charcoal from stake-hole cut into the base of subrectangular charcoal production pit	948 ± 36	AD 1029–1152 one sigma AD 1019–1165 two sigma
Beta-194572	Kilmaniheen West (site AR05), Co. Kerry	Oak (*Quercus*) charcoal from primary fill of subrectangular charcoal production pit	1080 ± 60	AD 900–1010 one sigma AD 810–1030 two sigma

Lab code	Site	Sample/context	Yrs BP	Calibrated date ranges
Beta-207373	Kilmaniheen West (site AR05), Co. Kerry	Alder (*Alnus*) and hazel (*Corylus*) charcoal from primary fill of subrectangular/oval charcoal production pit	980 ± 40	AD 1010–1040 one sigma AD 990–1160 two sigma
SUERC-9818	Mayfield site 15, Co. Kildare	Oak (*Quercus*) charcoal from subcircular charcoal production pit	1195 ± 35	AD 770–890 one sigma AD 690–950 two sigma
Beta-201037	Mondaniel 1, Co. Cork	Oak (*Quercus*) charcoal from upper fill of circular charcoal production pit	400 ± 60	AD 1440–1620 one sigma AD 1420–1640 two sigma
Beta-201038	Mondaniel 2, Co. Cork	Oak (*Quercus*) charcoal from lower fill of circular charcoal production pit	630 ± 50	AD 1290–1400 one sigma AD 1280–1420 two sigma
UB-6937	Monganstown 1, Co. Westmeath	Oak (*Quercus*) charcoal from primary fill of subrectangular charcoal production pit	1050 ± 29	AD 977–1020 one sigma AD 898–1026 two sigma
UB-6938	Monganstown 1, Co. Westmeath	Oak (*Quercus*) charcoal from primary fill of subrectangular charcoal production pit	1056 ± 30	AD 908–1020 one sigma AD 896–1025 two sigma
Beta-177441	Newcastle 2, Co. Meath	Oak (*Quercus*) charcoal from lower fill of subrectangular charcoal production pit	850 ± 40	AD 1170–1240 one sigma AD 1050–1270 two sigma
UCD-0114	Richmond site Q, Co. Tipperary	Charcoal (no record of species) from possible subrectangular charcoal production pit	370 ± 66	AD 1443–1636 one sigma AD 1423–1657 two sigma
Beta-177430	Rossan 3, Co. Meath	Oak (*Quercus*) charcoal from lower fill of subrectangular charcoal production pit	840 ± 60	AD 1160–1260 one sigma AD 1030–1280 two sigma
UBA-9157	Russagh 4, Co. Offaly	Oak (*Quercus*) charcoal from primary fill of subrectangular charcoal production pit	983 ± 27	AD 1017–1147 one sigma AD 994–1153 two sigma
UBA-9158	Russagh 4, Co. Offaly	Oak (*Quercus*) charcoal (bark) from primary fill of circular charcoal production pit	898 ± 24	AD 1048–1181 one sigma AD 1042–1211 two sigma
UB-7222	Tincurry, Co. Tipperary	Oak (*Quercus*) charcoal from upper fill of irregular charcoal production pit	899 ± 29	AD 1047–1185 one sigma AD 1040–1212 two sigma

Appendix 1

Lab code	Site	Sample/context	Yrs BP	Calibrated date ranges
UB-7223	Tincurry, Co. Tipperary	Oak (*Quercus*) charcoal from spread overlying a possible charcoal production mound (spread)	347 ± 25	AD 1485–1631 one sigma AD 1463–1635 two sigma
UBA-9372	Tonaphort 3, Co. Westmeath	Oak (*Quercus*) charcoal from primary fill of rectangular charcoal production pit	1160 ± 33	AD 782–944 one sigma AD 777–970 two sigma

References

Aaron, J R 1980 *The Production of Wood Charcoal in Great Britain*. HMSO, London.

AFM = O'Donovan, J (ed. & trans.) 1848–51 *Annála Rioghachta Éireann: Annals of the Kingdom of Ireland by the Four Masters, from the earliest period to the year 1616*, Vol. 2 [1998 reprint]. De Búrca Rare Books, Dublin.

Andersson, E B 2007 'Engendering central places: some aspects of the organisation of textile production during the Viking Age', *in* A Rast-Eicher & R Windler (eds), *NESAT IX: Archäologische Textilfunde—Archaeological Textiles: Braunwald 18–21 Mai 2005*, 148–53. Unterstutzung des Lotteriefonds der Kanton Glarus, Ennenda.

Apel, J 2001 *Daggers, Knowledge and Power: the social aspects of flint-dagger technology in Scandinavia, 2350–1500 cal. BC*. University of Uppsala, Uppsala.

Apel, J 2008 'Knowledge, know-how and raw material—the production of Late Neolithic flint daggers in Scandinavia', *Journal of Archaeological Method and Theory*, Vol. 15, No. 1, 91–111.

Archaeological Services Durham University 2009 'APPENDIX 10A. Pollen Analysis: Archaeological Services Durham University (ASDU)', *in* S J Linnane & J Kinsella, *Report on the Archaeological Excavation of Baronstown 1, Co. Meath* (http://www.m3motorway.ie/Archaeology/Section2/Baronstown1/file, 16723,en.pdf, accessed November 2009).

Ardron, P A & Rotherham, I D 1999 'Types of charcoal hearth and the impact of charcoal and whitecoal production on woodland vegetation', *The Peak District Journal of Natural History and Archaeology*, Vol. 1, 35–47.

Armstrong, L 1979 *Woodcolliers and Charcoal Burning*. Weald & Downland Open Air Museum, Singleton, Sussex.

AU = Mac Airt, S & Mac Niocaill, G (eds & trans) 1983 *The Annals of Ulster (to AD 1131), Part 1, Text and Translation*. Dublin Institute for Advanced Studies, Dublin.

Baxter, J E 2005 *The Archaeology of Childhood: children, gender and material culture*. Altamira Press, Walnut Creek, California.

Bayley, D 2006 'Site 127, Carn More 5, Faughart. Bronze Age cemetery', *in* I Bennett (ed.), *Excavations 2003: summary accounts of archaeological excavations in Ireland*, 340–1. Wordwell, Bray.

Beese, A (in prep.) 'Geology of the stone axes and other macro-tools', *in* R Cleary (ed.), *Neolithic Settlement in North Munster: archaeological excavation at Tullahedy, Co. Tipperary*.

Binchy, D 1978 *Corpus Iuris Hibernici*, Vol. 2. Dublin Institute for Advanced Studies, Dublin.

Bolger, T 2002 'Three sites on the M1 motorway at Rathmullan, Co. Meath', *Ríocht na Midhe*, Vol. 13, 8–17.

Bourke, C 1980 'Early Irish hand bells', *Journal of the Royal Society of Antiquaries of Ireland*, Vol. 110, 52–65.

Bourke, C 2008 'Early ecclesiastical hand bells in Ireland and Britain', *Journal of the Antique Metalware Society*, Vol. 16, 22–8.

Breen, T 2007a *Preliminary Report. Archaeological Excavations (A003/019, E3491), Raheenagurren West Sites 27, 28 and 29. N11 Gorey to Arklow Link, Co. Wexford*. Unpublished report for Valerie J Keeley Ltd.

Breen, T C 2007b 'Beside the rath: excavations at Raheenagurren, Co. Wexford', *in* J

O'Sullivan & M Stanley (eds), *New Routes to the Past*, 1–10. Archaeology and the National Roads Authority Monograph Series No. 4. National Roads Authority, Dublin.

Brindley, A L 1980 'The Cinerary Urn tradition in Ireland—an alternative interpretation', *Proceedings of the Royal Irish Academy*, Vol. 80C, 197–206.

Brindley, A L 1999 'Irish Grooved Ware', *in* R Cleal & A MacSween (eds), *Grooved Ware in Britain and Ireland*, 23–35. Neolithic Studies Group Seminar Papers 3. Oxbow, Oxford.

Brindley, A L 2007a *The Dating of Food Vessels and Urns in Ireland*. Bronze Age Studies 7. Department of Archaeology, National University of Ireland, Galway.

Brindley, A L 2007b 'Prehistoric pottery from Knockhouse Lower, Co. Waterford (03E1033)', *in* A Richardson & P Johnston, 'Excavation of a Middle Bronze Age settlement site at Knockhouse Lower, Co. Waterford', *Decies*, Vol. 63, 12–13.

Brindley, A L & Lanting, J 1989/90 'Radiocarbon dates for Neolithic single burials', *Journal of Irish Archaeology*, Vol. 5, 1–7.

Bronk Ramsey, C 2005 *OxCal Program v.3.10* (http://www.rlaha.ox.ac.uk/O/oxcal.php).

Bronk Ramsey, C 2009 *OxCal Program v.4.1* (https://c14.arch.ox.ac.uk/oxcal/OxCal.html).

Buckley, L, Cross May, S, Gregory, N et al. 2005 'Catalogue of finds', *in* M Gowen, J Ó Néill & M Phillips (eds), *The Lisheen Mine Archaeological Project, 1996–8*, 311–28. Wordwell, Bray.

Buick, G R 1893 'The Crannog of Moylarg', *Journal of the Royal Society of Antiquaries of Ireland*, Vol. 23, 27–43.

Campbell, C 2008 'Heathtown. Pit with Grooved Ware', *in* I Bennett (ed.), *Excavations 2005: summary accounts of archaeological excavations in Ireland*, 292. Wordwell, Bray.

Carlin, N 2008 'Ironworking and production', *in* N Carlin, L Clarke & F Walsh, *The Archaeology of Life and Death in the Boyne Floodplain: the linear landscape of the M4*, 87–112. NRA Scheme Monographs 2. National Roads Authority, Dublin..

Carroll, J, Ryan, F & Wiggins, K 2008 *Archaeological Excavations at Glebe South and Darcystown, Balrothery, Co. Dublin*. Balrothery Excavations, Vol. 2. Judith Carroll and Co. Ltd, Dublin.

Carver, M 2008 *Portmahomack: monastery of the Picts*. Edinburgh University Press, Edinburgh.

Case, H 1961 'Irish Neolithic pottery: distribution and sequence', *Proceedings of the Prehistoric Society*, Vol. 9, 174–233.

Case, H 1993 'Beakers: deconstruction and after', *Proceedings of the Prehistoric Society*, Vol. 59, 241–68.

Case, H 1995 'Irish Beakers in their European context', *in* J Waddell & E Shee Twohig (eds), *Ireland in the Bronze Age*, 14–29. Stationery Office, Dublin.

Chadwick, E 1989 *The Craft of Hand Spinning*. Batsford, London.

Channing, J 1993 'Aughrim. Wedge tomb', *in* I Bennett (ed.), *Excavations 1992: summary accounts of archaeological excavations in Ireland*, 4. Wordwell, Bray.

Clarke, D L 1970 *Beaker Pottery of Great Britain and Ireland*. Gulbenkian Archaeological Series. Cambridge University Press, Cambridge.

Clarke, L & Carlin, N 2008 'Living with the dead at Johnstown 1: an enclosed burial, settlement and industrial site', *in* N Carlin, L Clarke & F Walsh, *The Archaeology of Life and Death in the Boyne Floodplain: the linear landscape of the M4*, 55–85. NRA Scheme Monographs 2. National Roads Authority, Dublin.

Cleary, R M 1983 'The ceramic assemblage', *in* M J O'Kelly, R M Cleary & D Lehane, *Newgrange, Co. Meath, Ireland: the Late Neolithic/Beaker Period settlement* (ed. C O'Kelly), 58–117. British Archaeological Reports, International Series 190. Oxford.

Cleary, R M 1995 'Later Bronze Age settlement and prehistoric burials, Lough Gur, Co. Limerick', *Proceedings of the Royal Irish Academy*, Vol. 95C, 1–92.

Cleary, R M 2008 'The pottery from site A (Chancellorsland)', *in* M Doody, *The Ballyhoura Hills Project*, 259–303. Discovery Programme Monograph 7. Wordwell, Bray.

Cleary, R (ed.) (in prep.) *Neolithic Settlement in North Munster: archaeological excavation at Tullahedy, Co. Tipperary*.

Collins, A E P 1952 'Excavations in the sandhills at Dundrum, Co. Down, 1950–51', *Ulster Journal of Archaeology*, Vol. 15, 2–26.

Collins, A E P 1959 'Further investigations in the Dundrum sandhills', *Ulster Journal of Archaeology*, Vol. 22, 5–20.

Collins, A E P 1965 'Ballykeel Dolmen and Cairn, Co. Armagh', *Ulster Journal of Archaeology*, Vol. 28, 47–70.

Collins, A E P 1976 'Doey's Cairn, Ballymacaldrack, County Antrim', *Ulster Journal of Archaeology*, Vol. 39, 1–7.

Connolly, A 1999 *The Palaeoecology of Clara Bog, Co. Offaly*. Unpublished Ph.D thesis, Trinity College, Dublin.

Connon, A (forthcoming) 'History of the early medieval kingdom of Fir Tulach', *in* P Stevens & J Channing, *The Early Medieval Archaeology of Central Westmeath: excavations at Rochfort Demesne, Ballykilmore and Clonfad, on the N6/N52 Realignment Scheme*. NRA Scheme Monographs. National Roads Authority, Dublin.

Cooney, G 2000 'Recognising regionality in the Irish Neolithic', *in* A Desmond, M McCarthy, J Sheehan & E Shee Twohig (eds), *New Agendas in Irish Prehistory: papers in commemoration of Liz Anderson*, 49–65. Wordwell, Bray.

Cooney, G & Grogan, E 1994 *Irish Prehistory: a social perspective*. Wordwell, Bray.

Cotter, C 1993 'Western Stone Fort Project. Interim report 1992', *Discovery Programme Reports*, No. 1, 1–19. Royal Irish Academy/Discovery Programme, Dublin.

Cotter, C 1996 'Western Stone Fort Project: interim report', *Discovery Programme Reports*, No. 4, 1–14. Royal Irish Academy/Discovery Programme, Dublin.

Cotter, E 2005 'Bronze Age Ballybrowney, Co. Cork', *in* J O'Sullivan & M Stanley (eds), *Recent Archaeological Discoveries on National Road Schemes 2004*, 25–35. Archaeology and the National Roads Authority Monograph Series No. 2. National Roads Authority, Dublin.

Cotter, E 2008 'Cloonbaul/Kilbride. Late Neolithic timber circle, charcoal-burning pits', *in* I Bennett (ed.), *Excavations 2005: summary accounts of archaeological excavations in Ireland*, 273. Wordwell, Bray.

Coughlan, T 2007 'The enigma of Cappydonnell Big', *Seanda*, No. 2, 16–17.

Coughlan, T 2009a *Report on the archaeological excavation of Kilbeggan South 3, Co. Westmeath*. Unpublished excavation report by Irish Archaeological Consultancy Ltd.

Coughlan, T 2009b 'The continuing enigma of Cappydonnell Big', *Seanda*, No. 4, 42–4.

Crew, P 1986 'Bryn y Castell Hillfort—a late prehistoric iron working settlement in north-west Wales', *in* B G Scott & H Cleere (eds), *The Crafts of the Blacksmith: essays presented to R F Tylecote at the 1984 Symposium of the UISPP Comité pour la Sidéurgie Ancienne*, 91–100. UISPP Comité pour la Sidéurgie Ancienne/Ulster Museum, Belfast.

Crew, P 1996 *Bloom Refining and Smithing Slags and Other Residues*. Historical Metallurgy Society Archaeology Datasheet No. 6 (http://hist-met.org/hmsdatasheet06.pdf, accessed November 2009).

Crew, P & Mighall, T M (forthcoming) 'The fuel supply and woodland management at a 14th century bloomery in Snowdonia, a multi-disciplinary approach', *in* H A Veldhuijzen & J Humphris (eds), *The World of Iron: proceedings of a conference at the National History Museum, 2009*. Archetype Publications, London.

Crowfoot, G M 1931 *Methods of Hand Spinning in Egypt and the Sudan*. Bankfield Museum Series 2, No. 12. Bankfield Museum, Halifax.

Cunliffe, B 1984 *Danebury: an Iron Age hillfort in Hampshire: Vol. 2. The excavations, 1969–1978: the finds*. Council for British Archaeology, London.

Danaher, E 2004 *Report on the Excavation of an Early Bronze Age Pit at Barnagore 4, Ballincollig, Co. Cork*. Unpublished report to Cork County Council on behalf of Archaeological Consultancy Services Ltd.

Danaher, E, Kane, E & Kenny, N 2008a *Report on the archaeological excavation of Kilcotton 1, Co. Laois*. Unpublished excavation report by Archaeological Consultancy Services Ltd.

Danaher, E, Kane, E & Kenny, N 2008b *Report on the archaeological excavation of Kilcotton 2, Co. Laois*. Unpublished excavation report by Archaeological Consultancy Services Ltd.

Davies, O 1950 'Excavations at Island MacHugh', *Supplement to the Proceedings and Reports of the Belfast Natural History and Philosophical Society*.

Doody, M G 1987 'Ballyveelish, Co. Tipperary', *in* R M Cleary, M F Hurley & E A Twohig (eds), *Archaeological Excavation on the Cork–Dublin Gas Pipeline (1981–82)*, 9–35. Cork Archaeological Studies No. 1. Department of Archaeology, University College Cork.

Doody, M 2008 *The Ballyhoura Hills Project*. Discovery Programme Monograph 7. Wordwell, Bray.

Duffy, C 2002 'Hill of Rath, prehistoric complex, Co. Louth', *in* I Bennett (ed.), *Excavations 2000: summary accounts of archaeological excavations in Ireland*, 231–3. Wordwell, Bray.

Duffy, C 2005 *Excavation Report, Site 4, Steelstown, Co. Dublin. N7 Naas Road-Widening and Interchanges scheme*. Unpublished report for Irish Archaeological Consultancy Ltd.

Dunne, L 1998 'Late Bronze Age burials in County Kerry', *Archaeology Ireland*, Vol. 12, No. 2, 4.

Durrani, N 2010 'World's oldest cloth', *Current World Archaeology*, Issue 39, 10–11.

Earwood, C 1991/2 'A radiocarbon date for the Early Bronze Age wooden polypod bowls', *Journal of Irish Archaeology*, Vol. 4, 27–8.

Edwards, N 1990 *The Archaeology of Early Medieval Ireland*. Routledge, London & New York.

Egan, O 2009 'Ringing out the old: reconstructing the bell of Clonfad', *Seanda*, No. 4, 52–3.

Elliot, R 2008 *AR146 Paulstown 2 (E3632). Archaeological Resolution Report, N9/N10 Kilcullen to Waterford Scheme. Phase 4b: Rathclogh to Powerstown*. Unpublished interim report on behalf of Kilkenny County Council.

Eogan, G 1963 'A Neolithic habitation-site and megalithic tomb in Townleyhall townland, Co. Louth', *Journal of the Royal Society of Antiquaries of Ireland*, Vol. 93, 37–81.

Eogan, G 1984 *Excavations at Knowth (1)*. Royal Irish Academy Monographs in Archaeology. Royal Irish Academy, Dublin.

Eogan, G & Roche, H 1997 *Excavations at Knowth (2)*. Royal Irish Academy Monographs in Archaeology. Royal Irish Academy, Dublin.

Eogan, J 1999 'Recent excavations at Bettystown, Co. Meath', *Irish Association of Professional Archaeologists Newsletter*, Vol. 30, 9.

Evans, E E 1938 'A chambered cairn in Ballyedmond Park, County Down', *Ulster Journal of Archaeology*, Vol. 1, 49–58.

Evans, E E 1953 *Lyles Hill: a Late Neolithic site in County Antrim*. Archaeological Research Publications (Northern Ireland) No. 2. HMSO, Belfast.

Evans, E E & Davies, O 1934 'Excavation of a chambered horned cairn at Ballyalton, Co. Down', *Proceedings of the Belfast Natural History & Philosophical Society* (1933–4), 79–104.

Fanning, T 1981 'Excavation of an Early Christian cemetery and settlement at Reask, Co Kerry', *Proceedings of the Royal Irish Academy*, Vol. 81C, 67–172.

Ferguson, J R 2003 'An experimental test of the conservation of raw material in flintknapping skill acquisition', *Lithic Technology*, Vol. 28, 113–31.

Ferguson, J R 2008 'The when, where, and how of novices in craft production', *Journal of Archaeological Method and Theory*, Vol. 15, No. 1, 51–67.

FitzGerald, M 2006 'Archaeological discoveries on a new section of the N2 in counties Meath and Dublin', *in* J O'Sullivan & M Stanley (eds), *Settlement, Industry and Ritual*, 29–42. Archaeology and the National Roads Authority Monograph Series No. 3. National Roads Authority, Dublin.

Gailey, A & Harper, A E T 1984 'Excavation at Cathedral Hill, Armagh, 1968', *Ulster Journal of Archaeology*, Vol. 47, 147–39.

Gibson, A 1995 'First impressions: a review of Peterborough Ware in Wales', *in* I Kinnes & G Varndell (eds), *'Unbaked Urns of Rudely Shape': essays on British and Irish pottery for Ian Longworth*, 23–39. Oxbow Monograph 55. Oxbow, Oxford.

Gibson, A 2002 *Prehistoric Pottery in Britain and Ireland*. Tempus, Stroud.

Gillespie, R 2008 *Lowpark, Co Mayo*. Unpublished excavation report for Mayo County Council.

Gillespie, R F 2009 'A treasury in time around Charlestown, Co. Mayo', *Seanda*, No. 4, 8–11.

Gillespie, R F & Kerrigan, A (forthcoming) *Of Troughs and Tuyères: the archaeology of the N5 Charlestown Bypass*. NRA Scheme Monographs 6. National Roads Authority, Dublin.

Gowen, M 1988 *Three Irish Gas Pipelines: new archaeological evidence in Munster*. Wordwell, Bray.

Gowen, M & Ó Néill, J 2005 'Introduction', *in* M Gowen, J Ó Néill & M Phillips (eds), *The Lisheen Mine Archaeological Project, 1996–8*, 1–9. Wordwell, Bray.

Grogan, E 2004a 'The implications of Irish Neolithic houses', *in* I Shepherd & G Barclay (eds), *Scotland in Ancient Europe*, 103–14. Society of Antiquaries of Scotland, Edinburgh.

Grogan, E 2004b *The prehistoric pottery assemblage from Kilgobbin, Co. Dublin*. Unpublished report for Margaret Gowen & Co. Ltd.

Grogan, E 2004c 'Middle Bronze Age burial traditions in Ireland', *in* H Roche, E Grogan, J Bradley, J Coles & B Raftery (eds), *From Megaliths to Metals: essays in honour of George Eogan*, 61–71. Oxbow, Oxford.

Grogan, E 2005 *The North Munster Project, Vol. 1: the later prehistoric landscape of south-east Clare*. Discovery Programme Monograph No. 6. Wordwell, Bray.

Grogan, E & Eogan, G 1987 'Lough Gur excavations by Seán P Ó Ríordáin: further

Neolithic and Beaker habitations on Knockadoon', *Proceedings of the Royal Irish Academy*, Vol. 87C, 299–506.

Grogan, E & Roche, H 2004a *The Prehistoric Pottery from Kilbane, Castletroy, Co. Limerick*. Unpublished report for Eachtra Archaeology Ltd.

Grogan, E & Roche, H 2004b *The Prehistoric Pottery from Site 6B, Priestsnewtown, Greystones, Co. Wicklow*. Unpublished report for Judith Carroll and Co. Ltd.

Grogan, E & Roche, H 2005a *The Prehistoric Pottery from Balregan 1, Co. Louth (03E0157)*. Unpublished report for Irish Archaeological Consultancy Ltd.

Grogan, E & Roche, H 2005b *The Prehistoric Pottery from Newtownbalregan 2, Co. Louth*. Unpublished report for Irish Archaeological Consultancy Ltd.

Grogan, E & Roche, H 2006a *The Prehistoric Pottery from Carn More 5, Co. Louth (03E0873)*. Unpublished report for Irish Archaeological Consultancy Ltd.

Grogan, E & Roche, H 2006b *The prehistoric pottery from Pit C12, Mitchelstown, Co. Cork (04E1071). N8 Mitchelstown Relief Road*. Unpublished report for Eachtra Archaeological Projects.

Grogan, E & Roche, H 2008a *The M7/M8 Portlaoise to Cullahill Scheme. The Prehistoric Pottery from Parknahown 5, Co. Laois (E2170)*. Unpublished report for Archaeological Consultancy Services Ltd.

Grogan, E & Roche, H 2008b *N11 Gorey–Arklow Link Road, Co. Wexford. The Prehistoric Pottery Assemblage from Raheenagurren West, Co. Wexford (A003/019, E3491)*. Unpublished report for Valerie J Keeley Ltd.

Grogan, E & Roche, H 2008c 'The prehistoric pottery assemblage from Darcystown 1, Balrothery, Co. Dublin (03E0067/ 03E0067 extension)', *in* J Carroll, F Ryan & K Wiggins, *Archaeological Excavations at Glebe South and Darcystown, Balrothery, Co. Dublin*, 48–63. Balrothery Excavations, Vol. 2. Judith Carroll and Co. Ltd, Dublin.

Grogan, E & Roche, H 2008d 'The prehistoric pottery assemblage from Darcystown 2, Balrothery, Co. Dublin (04E0741)', *in* J Carroll, F Ryan & K Wiggins, *Archaeological Excavations at Glebe South and Darcystown, Balrothery, Co. Dublin*, 85–101. Balrothery Excavations, Vol. 2. Judith Carroll and Co. Ltd, Dublin.

Grogan, E & Roche, H 2008e 'Appendix 2.2. The prehistoric pottery', *in* F Walsh, *N6 Kinnegad–Athlone Road Scheme: Phase 2, Kilbeggan–Athlone Dual Carriageway. Site A016/051; E2677: Tober 1, Co. Offaly*. Unpublished report on behalf of Westmeath County Council.

Grogan, E & Roche, H 2009a *The Prehistoric Pottery from Blackglen, Balally, Co. Dublin (03E0291)*. Unpublished report for Irish Archaeological Consultancy Ltd.

Grogan, E & Roche, H 2009b *The prehistoric pottery assemblage from Paulstown 2, Co. Kilkenny (AR146, E3632). N9/N10 Rathclogh to Powerstown*. Unpublished report for Irish Archaeological Consultancy Ltd.

Grogan, E & Roche, H 2009c 'Prehistoric pottery', *in* M McQuade, B Molloy & C Moriarty, *In the Shadow of the Galtees: archaeological excavations along the N8 Cashel to Mitchelstown Road Scheme*, 288–314. NRA Scheme Monographs 4. National Roads Authority, Dublin.

Grogan, E & Roche, H 2009d *The prehistoric pottery from Monamintra, Co. Waterford*. Unpublished report for Daniel Noonan Archaeological Consultancy.

Grogan, E & Roche, H 2010a 'An assessment of middle Bronze Age domestic pottery in Ireland', *in* G Cooney, K Becker, J Coles, M Ryan & S Sievers (eds), *Relics of Old Decency:*

archaeological studies in later prehistory. A Festschrift for Barry Raftery, 127–36. Wordwell, Dublin.

Grogan, E & Roche, H 2010b 'A Bronze Age funerary crisis', *in* M Davies, U MacConville & G Cooney (eds), *A Grand Gallimaufry: collected in honour of Nick Maxwell*, 15–17. Wordwell, Dublin.

Grogan, E, O'Donnell, L & Johnston, P 2007 *The Bronze Age Landscapes of the Pipeline to the West: an integrated archaeological and environmental assessment*. Wordwell, Bray.

Hagen, I 2004 *Archaeological Excavations Report. Phase 3 Development, Kilgobbin, Co. Dublin*. Unpublished report for Margaret Gowen & Co. Ltd.

Hall, V A 2003 'Vegetation history of mid- to western Ireland in the 2nd millennium AD; fresh evidence from tephra-dated palynological investigations', *Vegetation History and Archaeobotany*, Vol. 12, 1–17.

Hart, C E 1968 'Charcoal-burning in the Royal Forest of Dean', *Bulletin of the Historical Metallurgy Group*, Vol. 2, No. 1, 33–9.

Hartnett, P J 1957 'Excavation of a passage grave at Fourknocks, Co. Meath', *Proceedings of the Royal Irish Academy*, Vol. 58C, 197–277.

Hartnett, P J 1971 'The excavation of two tumuli at Fourknocks (sites II and III), Co. Meath', *Proceedings of the Royal Irish Academy*, Vol. 71C, 35–89.

Hartnett, P J & Eogan, G 1964 'Feltrim Hill, Co. Dublin: a Neolithic and Early Christian site', *Journal of the Royal Society of Antiquaries of Ireland*, Vol. 94, 1–37.

Hartwell, B 1998 'The Ballynahatty Complex', *in* A Gibson & D Simpson (eds), *Prehistoric Ritual and Religion*, 32–44. Sutton Publishing Ltd, Stroud.

Haustein, M, Roewer, G, Krbetschek, M R & Pernicka, E 2003 'Dating archaeometallurgical slags using thermoluminescence', *Archaeometry*, Vol. 45, No. 3, 519–30.

Hayen, H 1987 'New light on the history of transport', *Endeavour* (new series), Vol. 11, No. 4, 209–15.

Healy, P 1972 *Supplementary Survey of Ancient Monuments at Glendalough, Co. Wicklow*. Office of Public Works, Dublin.

Heckett, E 1991 'Textiles in archaeology', *Archaeology Ireland*, Vol. 5, No. 2, 11–13.

Heckett, E 2007 'Late Bronze Age textiles, hair and fibre remains, and spindle whorls from Killymoon, Northern Ireland', *in* A Rast-Eicher & R Windler (eds), *NESAT IX: Archäologische Textilfunde—Archaeological Textiles: Braunwald 18–21 Mai 2005*, 28–34. Unterstutzung des Lotteriefonds der Kanton Glarus, Ennenda.

Heery, A 1998 *The Vegetation History of the Irish Midlands: palaeoecological reconstructions of two lake sites adjacent to two eskers*. Unpublished Ph.D thesis, Trinity College, Dublin.

Hencken, H O'N 1938 'Cahercommaun, a stone fort in County Clare', *Journal of the Royal Society of Antiquaries of Ireland*, Vol. 68, 1–82.

Hencken, H O'N 1942 'Ballinderry Crannog No. 2', *Proceedings of the Royal Irish Academy*, Vol. 47C, 1–76.

Hencken, H O'N 1950 'Lagore crannog: an Irish royal residence of the 7th to 10th centuries AD', *Proceedings of the Royal Irish Academy*, Vol. 53C, 1–247.

Henry, S 1934 'A find of prehistoric pottery at Knockaholet, Parish of Loughguile, Co. Antrim', *Journal of the Royal Society of Antiquaries of Ireland*, Vol. 64, 264–5.

Henshall, A S 1950 'Textiles and weaving appliances in prehistoric Britain', *Proceedings of the Prehistoric Society*, Vol. 16, 130–63.

Herity, M 1982 'Irish decorated Neolithic pottery', *Proceedings of the Royal Irish Academy*, Vol. 82C, 247–404.

Herity, M 1987 'The finds from Irish court tombs', *Proceedings of the Royal Irish Academy*, Vol. 87C, 103–281.

Herring, I 1937 'The forecourt, Hanging Thorn Cairn, McIlwhan's Hill, Ballyutoag, Ligoneil', *Proceedings of the Belfast Natural History & Philosophical Society* (1936–7), 43–9.

Hibajene, S & Kalumiana, O 1996 *Manual for Charcoal Production in Earth Kilns in Zambia*. Department of Energy, Lusaka, Zambia.

Hull, G & Taylor, K 2006 'Archaeological sites on the route of the N21 Castleisland to Abbeyfeale Road Improvement Scheme, Co. Kerry', *Journal of the Kerry Archaeological and Historical Society*, Series 2, Vol. 6, 5–59.

Hurl, D 1996 'Killymoon Demesne, Co. Tyrone', *in* I Bennett (ed.), *Excavations 1995: summary accounts of archaeological excavations in Ireland*, 84. Wordwell, Bray.

Hurl, D 1998 'Ballybriest. Wedge tomb', *in* I Bennett (ed.), *Excavations 1997: summary accounts of archaeological excavations in Ireland*, 15. Wordwell, Bray.

International Labour Office 1985 *Fuelwood and Charcoal Preparation*. International Labour Office, Geneva.

Kavanagh, R 1973 'The Encrusted Urn in Ireland', *Proceedings of the Royal Irish Academy*, Vol. 73C, 507–617.

Kavanagh, R 1976 'Collared and Cordoned Urns in Ireland', *Proceedings of the Royal Irish Academy*, Vol. 76C, 293–403.

Kavanagh, R 1977 'Pygmy Cups in Ireland', *Journal of the Royal Society of Antiquaries of Ireland*, Vol. 107, 61–95.

Keeley, V J 1994 'The Heath, Heath. Area of archaeological potential', *in* I Bennett (ed.), *Excavations 1993: summary accounts of archaeological excavations in Ireland*, 50. Wordwell, Bray.

Kelleher, H (in prep.) 'The excavation', *in* R Cleary (ed.), *Neolithic Settlement in North Munster: archaeological excavation at Tullahedy, Co. Tipperary*.

Kelly, F 1998 *Early Irish Farming*. Early Irish Law Series 4. Dublin Institute for Advanced Studies, Dublin.

Kenny, N 2008 *Charcoal Production and Ironworking: a selection of sites from the M7/M8 motorway scheme in Co. Laois*. Unpublished research report for Archaeological Consultancy Services Ltd.

Kiely, J & Sutton, B 2007 'The new face of Bronze Age pottery', *in* J O'Sullivan & M Stanley (eds), *New Routes to the Past*, 25–33. Archaeology and the National Roads Authority Monograph Series No. 4. National Roads Authority, Dublin.

Kilbride-Jones, H E 1950 'The excavation of a composite early Iron Age monument with "henge" features at Lugg, Co. Dublin', *Proceedings of the Royal Irish Academy*, Vol. 53C, 311–32.

Kimaryo, B T & Ngereza, K I 1989 *Charcoal Production in Tanzania Using Improved Traditional Earth Kilns*. International Development Research Centre, Ottawa, Canada.

Knowles, W J 1905 'Spindle-whorls', *Ulster Journal of Archaeology*, Vol. 11, 1–9.

Laidlaw, G 2009 *Final Report on Excavations at Scart North, Co. Kilkenny (E3014). N9/N10 Dunkitt to Sheepstown*. Unpublished report for Valerie J Keeley Ltd.

Lalonde, D 2008 *Preliminary report on the excavation of a Bronze Age enclosure at Monamintra, Co. Waterford (07E0347)*. Unpublished report for Daniel Noonan Archaeological

Consultancy Ltd.

Lancy, D F 2008 *The Anthropology of Childhood: cherubs, chattel, changelings.* Cambridge University Press, Cambridge.

Lancy, D F & Grove, M (in press) 'Getting noticed: middle childhood in cross-cultural perspective', *Human Nature*, Vol. 21.

Lanting, J & van der Waals, D 1972 'British Beakers as seen from the Continent', *Helenium*, Vol. 12, 20–46.

Lawlor, H C 1925 *The Monastery of Saint Mochaoi of Nendrum.* The Belfast Natural History and Philosophical Society, Belfast.

Leask, H G & Price, L 1936 'The Labbacallee megalith, Co. Cork', *Proceedings of the Royal Irish Academy*, Vol. 43C, 77–101.

Lehane, J & Magee, I 2008 'Bronze Age burial at Ballynacarriga 3', *Seanda*, No. 3, 45.

Lennon, A M 2008 *Report on the archaeological excavation of Barnasallagh 1, Co. Laois.* Unpublished excavation report by Archaeological Consultancy Services Ltd.

Lennon, A M & Kane, E 2009 *Report on the archaeological excavation of Derrinsallagh 4, Co. Laois.* Unpublished excavation report by Archaeological Consultancy Services Ltd.

Linnane, S J 2006 *Final Report on Archaeological Excavation of Rath-Healy 1.* Unpublished report to Cork County Council on behalf of Archaeological Consultancy Services Ltd.

Linnane, S J & Kinsella, J 2007 'Fort Baronstown? Exploring the social role of an impressive ringfort on the M3', *Seanda*, No. 2, 57–9.

Linnane, S J & Kinsella, J 2009a 'Military lords and defensive beginnings: a preliminary assessment of the social role of an impressive rath at Baronstown', *in* M B Deevy & D Murphy (eds), *Places Along the Way: first findings on the M3*, 101–22. NRA Scheme Monographs 5. National Roads Authority, Dublin.

Linnane, S J & Kinsella, J 2009b *Report on the Archaeological Excavation of Baronstown 1, Co. Meath* (http://www.m3motorway.ie/Archaeology/Section2/Baronstown1/file, 16723, en.pdf, accessed November 2009).

Liversage, G D 1960 'A Neolithic site at Townleyhall, Co. Louth', *Journal of the Royal Society of Antiquaries of Ireland*, Vol. 90, 49–60.

Liversage, G D 1968 'Excavations at Dalkey Island, Co. Dublin, 1956–1959', *Proceedings of the Royal Irish Academy*, Vol. 66C, 53–233.

Longworth, I H 1984 *Collared Urns of the Bronze Age in Great Britain and Ireland.* Cambridge University Press, Cambridge.

Lucas, A T 1972 'Prehistoric block-wheels from Doogarymore, Co. Roscommon, and Timahoe, Co. Kildare', *Journal of the Royal Society of Antiquaries of Ireland*, Vol. 102, 19–49.

Lynn, C J 1977 'Recent excavations in Armagh City: an interim report', *Seanchas Ard Mhacha*, Vol. 8, No. 2, 275–80.

Macalister, R A S 1929 'On some antiquities discovered upon Lambay', *Proceedings of the Royal Irish Academy*, Vol. 38C, 240–6.

McCabe, S 2004 'Lusk. Prehistoric burial-pit, pit and kiln', *in* I Bennett (ed.), *Excavations 2002: summary accounts of archaeological excavations in Ireland*, 176. Wordwell, Bray.

McConway, C 1998 'Tullahedy', *in* I Bennett (ed.), *Excavations 1997: summary accounts of archaeological excavations in Ireland*, 181. Wordwell, Bray.

McConway, C 2000 'Tullahedy', *in* I Bennett (ed.), *Excavations 1998: summary accounts of archaeological excavations in Ireland*, 203–4. Wordwell, Bray.

McCormack, F & Murray, E 2007 *Knowth and the Zooarchaeology of Early Christian Ireland.*

Excavations at Knowth 3. Royal Irish Academy, Dublin.

McCorry, M 1997 'Coarse pottery from Phase 3', *in* D Waterman, *Excavations at Navan Fort 1961–71* (ed. C J Lynn), 72–9. Northern Ireland Archaeological Monographs No. 1. The Stationery Office, Belfast.

McCracken, E 1971 *The Irish Woods since Tudor times.* Institute of Irish Studies, Queen's University, Belfast.

McDermott, C, Murray, C, Plunkett, G & Stanley, M 2002 'Of bogs, boats and bows: Irish Archaeological Wetland Unit Survey 2001', *Archaeology Ireland*, Vol. 16, No. 1, 28–31.

McDonnell, G 1995 *Iron Working Processes.* Historical Metallurgy Society Archaeology Datasheet No. 3 (http://hist-met.org/hmsdatasheet03.pdf, accessed November 2009).

McErlean, T & Crothers, N 2007 *Harnessing the Tide: the early medieval tide mills at Nendrum Monastery, Strangford Lough.* The Stationery Office/Environment and Heritage Service, Belfast.

MacLeod, R 2009 *Draft report on the archaeological excavation of Carrigatogher (site 2), Co. Tipperary.* Unpublished excavation report by Headland Archaeology Ltd.

McQuade, M 2005 'Archaeological excavation of a multi-period prehistoric settlement at Waterunder, Mell, Co. Louth', *County Louth Archaeological & Historical Journal*, Vol. 26, 31–66.

McQuade, M, Molloy, B & Moriarty, C 2009 *In the Shadow of the Galtees: archaeological excavations along the N8 Cashel to Mitchelstown Road Scheme.* NRA Scheme Monographs 4. National Roads Authority, Dublin.

Madden, A C 1969 'The Beaker wedge tomb at Moytirra, Co. Sligo', *Journal of the Royal Society of Antiquaries of Ireland*, Vol. 99, 151–9.

Mallory, J 1995 'Haughey's Fort and the Navan Complex in the Late Bronze Age', *in* J Waddell & E Shee Twohig (eds), *Ireland in the Bronze Age*, 73–89. Stationery Office, Dublin.

Mallory, J 1988 'Trial excavations at Haughey's Fort', *Emania*, Vol. 4, 5–20.

Mallory, J P 2004 'Wheels and carts', *in* B M Fagan (ed.), *The Seventy Great Inventions of the Ancient World*, 134–7. Thames & Hudson, London.

Mallory, J P & Hartwell, B 1984 'Donegore', *Current Archaeology*, Vol. 92, 271–5.

Megaw, J V S & Simpson, D D A 1979 *Introduction to British Prehistory.* Leicester University Press, Leicester.

Mighall, T M & Chambers, F M 1997 'Early ironworking and its impact on the environment: palaeoecological evidence from Bryn y Castell, Snowdonia, North Wales', *Proceedings of the Prehistoric Society*, Vol. 63, 199–219.

Mighall, T M, Timberlake, S, Jenkins, D A & Grattan, J P 2006 'Using bog archives to reconstruct palaeopollution and vegetation change during the late Holocene', *in* I P Martini, A Martinez Cortizas & W Chesworth (eds), *Peatlands: evolution and records of environmental and climate changes*, 413–34. Elsevier, Amsterdam.

Mitchell, G F 1987 *The Shell Guide to Reading the Irish Landscape.* Country House, Dublin.

Monk, M 1995 'A tale of two ringforts: Lisleagh I and II', *Journal of the Cork Historical and Archaeological Society*, Vol. 100, 105–16.

Monteith, J 2007 *Report on Excavations at Scart 1, Co. Kilkenny (E3014). N9/N10 Dunkitt to Sheepstown.* Unpublished report for Valerie J Keeley Ltd.

Moore, C 2008 'Old routes to new research: the Edercloon wetland excavations in County Longford', *in* J O'Sullivan & M Stanley (eds), *Roads, Rediscovery and Research*, 1–12.

Archaeology and the National Roads Authority Monograph Series No. 5. National Roads Authority, Dublin.

Moore, C (forthcoming) Final publication on the N4 excavations. NRA Scheme Monographs. National Roads Authority, Dublin.

Moore, D G 2007 'Neolithic segmented enclosure, Early Bronze Age activity', *in* I Bennett (ed.), *Excavations 2004: summary accounts of archaeological excavations in Ireland*, 143–6. Wordwell, Bray.

Moore, P D, Webb, J A & Collinson, M E 1991 *Pollen Analysis*. Blackwell Scientific Publications, Oxford.

Mount, C 1995 'New research on Irish Early Bronze Age cemeteries', *in* J Waddell & E Shee Twohig (eds), *Ireland in the Bronze Age*, 97–112. Stationery Office, Dublin.

Murphy, D 2003 'Excavations carried out on the site of the new Bord Fáilte office in 1999–2000', *in* H King (ed.), *Clonmacnoise Studies. Volume 2: Seminar Papers 1998*, 1–34. Wordwell, Bray.

Murphy, D 2004 *Draft report on the archaeological excavation of Hardwood 3, Co. Meath*. Unpublished excavation report by Archaeological Consultancy Services Ltd.

Murray, C, Stanley, M, McDermott, C & Moore, C 2002 'Sticks and stones: Wetland Unit Survey 2002', *Archaeology Ireland*, Vol. 16, No. 4, 16–19.

Murray, R 2008 'Iron masters of the Caledonians', *Current Archaeology*, Vol. 18, No. 212, 21–5.

Nassaney, M S 1996 'The role of chipped stone in political economy of social ranking', *in* G H Odell (ed.), *Stone Tools: theoretical insights into human prehistory*, 181–224. Plenum Press, New York.

Nicholls, J (forthcoming) 'Geophysical survey adjacent to Clonfad monastic site WM032:089, N6 Kinnegad–Kilbeggan Road Scheme, Co. Westmeath', *in* P Stevens & J Channing, *The Early Medieval Archaeology of Central Westmeath: excavations at Rochfort Demesne, Ballykilmore and Clonfad, on the N6/N52 Realignment Scheme* (on CD–ROM). NRA Scheme Monographs. National Roads Authority, Dublin.

Nolan, J 2006 'Excavation of a children's burial ground at Tonybaun, Ballina, County Mayo', *in* J O'Sullivan & M Stanley (eds), *Settlement, Industry and Ritual*, 89–101. Archaeology and the National Roads Authority Monograph Series No. 3. National Roads Authority, Dublin.

Nyberg, G G 1990 'Spinning implements of the Viking Age from Elisenhof in the light of ethnological studies', *in* P Walton & J P Wild (eds), *Textiles in Northern Archaeology: NESAT II*, 73–84. Archetype Publications, London.

Oakley, G E & Hall, A D 1979 'Spindle whorls', *in* J H Williams, *St Peter's Street, Northampton: excavations 1973–1976*, 286–9. Northampton Development Corporation, Northampton.

O'Brien, R 1993 *A Study of Irish Perforated/Unperforated Stone Discs*. Unpublished MA thesis, University College Cork.

O'Brien, R 2004 *Perforated Lead Objects from Woodstown 6, Co. Waterford*. Unpublished report to Waterford County Council on behalf of Archaeological Consultancy Services Ltd.

O'Brien, R 2009a 'Spindle-whorls', *in* M McQuade, M Molloy & C Moriarty, *In the Shadow of the Galtees: archaeological excavations along the N8 Cashel to Mitchelstown Road Scheme*, 346–8. NRA Scheme Monographs 4. National Roads Authority, Dublin.

O'Brien, R 2009b *Tober Spindle Whorl, Co. Offaly*. Unpublished report to Offaly County Council on behalf of Irish Archaeological Consultancy Ltd.

O'Brien, R & Russell, I 2005 'The Hiberno-Scandinavian site at Woodstown 6, County Waterford', *in* J O'Sullivan & M Stanley (eds), *Recent Archaeological Discoveries on National Road Schemes 2004*, 111–24. Archaeology and the National Roads Authority Monograph Series No. 2. National Roads Authority, Dublin.

O'Brien, R, Quinney, P & Russell, I 2005 'Preliminary report on archaeological excavation and finds retrieval strategy of the Hiberno-Scandinavian site at Woodstown 6, County Waterford', *Decies*, Vol. 61, 13–122.

O'Brien, W 1995 'Ross Island—the beginning', *Archaeology Ireland*, Vol. 9, No. 1, 24–7.

O'Brien, W 1996 *Bronze Age Copper Mining in Britain and Ireland*. Shire Archaeology, Princes Risborough.

O'Brien, W 1999 *Sacred Ground: megalithic tombs in coastal south-west Ireland*. Bronze Age Studies 4. Department of Archaeology, National University of Ireland, Galway.

O'Callaghan, N 2006 'Kilbane, Castletroy. Bronze Age flat cemetery and *fulachta fiadh*', *in* I Bennett (ed.), *Excavations 2003: summary accounts of archaeological excavations in Ireland*, 309–10. Wordwell, Bray.

OCarroll, E 2008 *Specialist report on the wood and charcoal analysis from Contract 2 of the M7 Portlaoise to Castletown/M8 Portlaoise to Culahill Motorway Scheme*. Unpublished specialist report for Archaeological Consultancy Services Ltd.

OCarroll, E 2009 *Report on the archaeological excavation of Russagh 4, Co. Offaly*. Unpublished excavation report by Irish Archaeological Consultancy Ltd.

O'Connor, D J, McDermott, C, Stanley, M & McGowan, L 2004 *N6 Kinnegad to Athlone Dual Carriageway. Advance Archaeological Investigation. Contract 2: Tyrrellspass to Kilbeggan*. Unpublished report commissioned by Westmeath County Council & the NRA.

Ó Donnchadha, B 2003 *M1 Dundalk Western Bypass. Site 116, Balregan 1 and 2*. Unpublished report for Irish Archaeological Consultancy Ltd.

O'Donnell, L 2007 'Environmental archaeology: identifying patterns of exploitation in the Bronze Age', *in* E Grogan, L O'Donnell & P Johnston, *The Bronze Age Landscapes of the Pipeline to the West: an integrated archaeological and environmental assessment*, 27–101. Wordwell, Bray.

Ó Drisceoil, C 2003 'Balgatheran Site 4. Late Neolithic ritual/settlement site, Co. Louth', *in* I Bennett (ed.), *Excavations 2001: summary accounts of archaeological excavations in Ireland*, 255–7. Wordwell, Bray.

Ó Droma, M 2008 'Archaeological investigations at Twomileborris, Co. Tipperary', *in* J O'Sullivan & M Stanley (eds), *Roads, Rediscovery and Research*, 45–58. Archaeology and the National Roads Authority Monograph Series No. 5. National Roads Authority, Dublin.

O'Hara, R 2003 *Draft report on the archaeological excavation of Newcastle 2, Co. Meath*. Unpublished excavation report by Archaeological Consultancy Services Ltd.

O'Kelly, M J 1951 'An Early Bronze Age ring-fort at Carrigillihy, Co. Cork', *Journal of the Cork Historical and Archaeological Society*, Vol. 56, 69–86.

O'Kelly, M J 1952 'St Gobnet's House, Ballyvourney, Co. Cork', *Journal of the Cork Historical and Archaeological Society*, Vol. 57, 18–40.

O'Kelly, M J 1960 'A wedge-shaped gallery grave at Baurnadomeeny, Co. Tipperary', *Journal of the Cork Historical and Archaeological Society*, Vol. 65, 85–115.

O'Kelly, M J   1962   'The excavations of two earthen ringforts at Garryduff, Co. Cork', *Proceedings of the Royal Irish Academy*, Vol. 63C, 17–125.

O'Neill, T & Kane, E   2008   *Report on the archaeological excavation of Trumra 3, Co. Laois*. Unpublished excavation report by Archaeological Consultancy Services Ltd.

Ó Ríordáin, B   1971   'Excavations at High Street and Winetavern Street, Dublin', *Medieval Archaeology*, Vol. 15, 73–85.

Ó Ríordáin, B & Waddell, J   1993   *The Funerary Bowls and Vases of the Irish Bronze Age*. Galway University Press, Galway.

Ó Ríordáin, S P   1942   'The excavation of a large earthen ring-fort at Garranes, Co. Cork', *Proceedings of the Royal Irish Academy*, Vol. 47C, 77–150.

Ó Ríordáin, S P   1951   'Lough Gur excavations: the Great Stone Circle (B) in Grange townland', *Proceedings of the Royal Irish Academy*, Vol. 54C, 37–74.

Ó Ríordáin, S P   1954   'Lough Gur excavations: Neolithic and Bronze Age houses on Knockadoon', *Proceedings of the Royal Irish Academy*, Vol. 56C, 297–459.

Ó Ríordáin, S P & de Valera, R   1952   'Excavations of a megalithic tomb at Ballyedmonduff, Co. Dublin', *Proceedings of the Royal Irish Academy*, Vol. 55C, 61–8.

Ó Ríordáin, S P & Ó h-Iceadha, G   1955   'Lough Gur excavations: the megalithic tomb', *Journal of the Royal Society of Antiquaries of Ireland*, Vol. 85, 34–50.

O'Sullivan, A   1990   'Wood in archaeology', *Archaeology Ireland*, Vol. 4, No. 2, 69–73.

O'Sullivan, A & Harney, L   2007   *The Early Medieval Archaeological Project: investigating the character of early medieval archaeological investigations, 1970–2002*. Unpublished report for the Heritage Council.

O'Sullivan, M   2005   *Duma na nGiall. The Mound of the Hostages, Tara*. School of Archaeology, UCD/Wordwell, Bray.

O'Sullivan, M & Downey, L   2009   'Charcoal production sites', *Archaeology Ireland*, Vol. 23, No. 4, 22–5.

Patterson, R   1956   'Hand distaffs from Lough Faughan, Lagore and Ballinderry crannogs', *Ulster Journal of Archaeology*, Vol. 18, 81–2.

Pétrequin, P & Pétrequin, A M   1993   *Écologie d'un Outil: la hache de pierre en Irian Jaya (Indonésie)*. CNRS, Paris.

Phelan, S   2007   '1903. Whitewell. Grooved Ware timber circle', *in* E Grogan, L O'Donnell & P Johnston, *The Bronze Age Landscapes of the Pipeline to the West: an integrated archaeological and environmental assessment*, 349–50. Wordwell, Bray.

Photos-Jones, E   2008a   'Analysis of metallurgical waste from Rossan VI, SASAA 91', *in* N Carlin, L Clarke & F Walsh, *The Archaeology of Life and Death in the Boyne Floodplain: the linear landscape of the M4* (on CD-ROM). NRA Scheme Monographs 2. National Roads Authority, Dublin.

Photos-Jones, E   2008b   'Analysis of metallurgical waste from Kinnegad II, SASAA 93', *in* N Carlin, L Clarke & F Walsh, *The Archaeology of Life and Death in the Boyne Floodplain: the linear landscape of the M4* (on CD-ROM). NRA Scheme Monographs 2. National Roads Authority, Dublin.

Photos-Jones, E   2008c   'Slag analysis for Johnstown 3, Appendix 2', *in* N Carlin, L Clarke & F Walsh, *The Archaeology of Life and Death in the Boyne floodplain: the linear landscape of the M4* (on CD-ROM). NRA Scheme Monographs 2. National Roads Authority, Dublin.

Piggott, S   1983   *The Earliest Wheeled Transport from the Atlantic Coast to the Caspian Sea*.

Thames & Hudson, London.

Piggott, S & Childe, V G 1932 'Neolithic pottery from Larne', *Proceedings of the Prehistoric Society of East Anglia*, Vol. 7, 62–6.

Pleiner, R 2000 *Iron in Archaeology: the European bloomery smelters*. Archaeologický Ústav AV CR, Praha.

Priest-Dorman, C 2000 *Medieval North European Spindles and Whorls* (http://www.cs.vassar.edu/~capriest/spindles.html, accessed February 2010).

Prim, G A 1855 'On the discovery of ogham monuments and other antiquities in the Raths of Dunbel, County of Kilkenny', *Proceedings and Transactions of the Kilkenny and South-East of Ireland Archaeological Society*, Vol. 2, 397–408.

Raftery, B 1969 'Freestone Hill, Co. Kilkenny: an Iron Age hillfort and Bronze Age cairn', *Proceedings of the Royal Irish Academy*, Vol. 68C, 1–108.

Raftery, B 1976 'Rathgall and Irish hillfort problems', *in* D Harding (ed.), *Hillforts: later prehistoric earthworks in Britain and Ireland*, 339–57. Academic Press, London.

Raftery, B 1995 'The conundrum of Irish Iron Age pottery', *in* B Raftery (ed.), *Sites and Sights of the Iron Age*, 149–56. Oxbow Monograph 56. Oxbow, Oxford.

Raftery, B 1996 *Trackway Excavations in the Mountdillon Bogs, Co. Longford, 1985–1991*. Transactions of the Irish Archaeological Wetland Unit, Vol. 3. Crannóg Publications, Dublin.

Raftery, J 1944 'A Neolithic burial in Co. Carlow', *Journal of the Royal Society of Antiquaries of Ireland*, Vol. 74, 61–2.

Reimer, P J, Baillie, M G L, Bard, E et al. 2004 'IntCal04 terrestrial radiocarbon age calibration, 0–26 cal kyr BP', *Radiocarbon*, Vol. 46, No. 3, 1029–58.

Richardson, Á & Johnston, P 2007 'Excavation of a Middle Bronze Age settlement site at Knockhouse Lower, Co. Waterford', *Decies*, Vol. 63, 1–17.

Roche, H 1995 *Style and Context for Grooved Ware in Ireland with Special Reference to the Assemblage at Knowth, Co. Meath*. Unpublished MA thesis, National University of Ireland, Galway.

Roche, H 1996 *The Prehistoric Pottery Assemblage from Longstone (Cullen), Co. Tipperary*. Unpublished report for *Dúchas*, the Heritage Service.

Roche, H 2004 'The dating of the embanked stone circle at Grange, Co. Limerick', *in* H Roche, E Grogan, J Bradley, J Coles & B Raftery (eds), *From Megaliths to Metals: essays in honour of George Eogan*, 109–16. Oxbow, Oxford.

Roche, H 2007 *The prehistoric pottery from Knockans, Rathlin Island, Co. Antrim*. Unpublished report for the Ulster Museum, Belfast.

Roche, H (forthcoming) 'The prehistoric pottery from Rathgall', *in* B Raftery, *The Hillfort at Rathgall*. Wordwell, Bray.

Roche, H & Grogan, E 2005a *N2 Finglas–Ashbourne. Kilshane, Co. Dublin (Site 5, O3E1359)*. Unpublished report for Cultural Resource Development Services Ltd.

Roche, H & Grogan, E 2005b *The N8 Rathcormac–Fermoy Bypass. The Prehistoric Pottery*. Unpublished report for Archaeological Consultancy Services Ltd.

Roche, H & Eogan, G 2007 'A re-assessment of the enclosure at Lugg, County Dublin, Ireland', *in* C Gosden, H Hamerow, P de Jersey & G Lock (eds), *Communities and Connections: essays in honour of Barry Cunliffe*, 154–68. Oxford University Press, Oxford.

Roche, H & Grogan, E 2008 *The Prehistoric Pottery from Corrstown, Co. Derry*. Unpublished report for Archaeological Consultancy Services Ltd.

Roche, H & Grogan, E 2009a *The Prehistoric Pottery from Ballynacarriga 3, Co. Tipperary (E2412). M8 Fermoy to Mitchelstown Bypass*. Unpublished report for Eachtra Archaeological Projects.

Roche, H & Grogan, E 2009b *The Prehistoric Pottery Assemblage from Paulstown 1, Co. Kilkenny (AR145, E3642). N9/N10 Rathclogh to Powerstown*. Unpublished report for Irish Archaeological Consultancy Ltd.

Roux, V & Blascó, P 2000 *Cornaline de l'Inde/Carnelian in India: from technical practices in Cambay to the techno-systems of the Indus*. Editions de la Maison des Sciences de l'Homme, Paris.

Roux, V, Bril, B & Dietrich, G 1995 'Skills and learning difficulties involved in stone knapping: the case of stone-bead knapping in Khambhat, India', *World Archaeology*, Vol. 27, No. 1, 63–87.

Roycroft, N 2005 'Around the bay on the Great North Road: the archaeology of the M1 Dundalk Western Bypass', *in* J O'Sullivan & M Stanley (eds), *Recent Archaeological Discoveries on National Road Schemes 2004*, 65–82. Archaeology and the National Roads Authority Monograph Series No. 2. National Roads Authority, Dublin.

Schlegel, A & Barry III, H 1980 'The evolutionary significance of adolescent initiation ceremonies', *American Ethnologist*, Vol. 7, 696–715.

Schubert, R 1957 *History of the British Iron and Steel Industry from c. 450 BC to AD 1775*. Routledge, London.

Scott, B 1990 *Early Irish Ironworking*. Ulster Museum, Belfast.

Sheehan, J 1990 'The excavation of a *fulacht fiadh* at Coarhamore, Valentia Island, Co. Kerry', *in* V Buckley (comp.), *Burnt Offerings*, 27–37. Wordwell, Dublin.

Sheridan, A 1993 'The manufacture, production and use of Irish Bowls and Vases', *in* B Ó Ríordáin & J Waddell, *The Funerary Bowls and Vases of the Irish Bronze Age*, 45–75. Galway University Press, Galway.

Sheridan, A 1995 'Irish Neolithic pottery: the story in 1995', *in* I Kinnes & G Varndell (eds), *'Unbaked Urns of Rudely Shape': essays on British and Irish pottery for Ian Longworth*, 3–21. Oxbow Monograph 55. Oxbow, Oxford.

Sillitoe, P 2004 'The Blade Runners', *British Archaeology*, Issue 79, 22–5.

Sleeman, M & Cleary, R 1987 'Pottery from Athgarret, Co. Kildare', *in* R Cleary, M Hurley & E Twohig (eds), *Archaeological Excavations on the Cork–Dublin Gas Pipeline (1981–82)*, 43–4. Cork Archaeological Studies No. 1. Department of Archaeology, University College Cork.

Smith, C S & Gnudi, M T (eds & trans) 1990 *The Pirotechnia of Vannoccio Biringuccio: the classic sixteenth-century treatise on metals and metallurgy*. Dover, New York.

Stanley, M, McDermott, C, Moore, C & Murray, C 2003 'Throwing off the yoke', *Archaeology Ireland*, Vol. 17, No. 2, 6–8.

Sternke, F 2001 *A Chip off the Old Rock: applying new approaches of lithic analysis to the lithic assemblage from the shell midden at Sparregård, Falster, Denmark*. Unpublished MA thesis, University College Cork.

Sternke, F 2005 'All are not hunters that knap the stone—a search for a woman's touch in Mesolithic stone tool production', *in* N Milner & P Woodman (eds), *Mesolithic Studies at the Beginning of the 21st Century*, 144–63. Oxbow, Oxford.

Sternke, F 2008a 'APPENDIX 6: Lithics Report', *in* T O'Neill & R O'Hara, *Report on the Archaeological Excavation of Skreen 2, Co. Meath* (http://www.m3motorway.ie/

Archaeology/Section2/Skreen2/file,16725,en.pdf, accessed November 2009).

Sternke, F 2008b 'APPENDIX 10: Lithics', *in* T O'Neill, *Report on the Archaeological Excavation of Skreen 3, Co. Meath* (http://www.m3motorway.ie/Archaeology/Section2/Skreen3/file,16726,en.pdf, accessed November 2009).

Sternke, F 2008c *Lithics Finds Report for E3727 Rathclough 2 (A032/106), Co. Kilkenny—N9/N10 Road Scheme, Knocktopher to Powerstown, Phase 4B*. Unpublished finds report for Irish Archaeological Consultancy Ltd on behalf of Kilkenny County Council.

Sternke, F 2008d *Lithics Finds Report for E3854 Holdenstown 5 (A032/131), Co. Kilkenny—N9/N10 Road Scheme, Knocktopher to Powerstown, Phase 4B*. Unpublished finds report for Irish Archaeological Consultancy Ltd on behalf of Kilkenny County Council.

Sternke, F 2009a 'APPENDIX 14: Lithics Report', *in* L Cagney, R O'Hara, G Kelleher & R Morkan, *Report on the Archaeological Excavation of Dowdstown 2, Co. Meath* (http://www.m3motorway.ie/Archaeology/Section2/Dowdstown2/file,16737,en.pdf, accessed November 2009).

Sternke, F 2009b 'APPENDIX 8: Lithics Finds Report for A008/022 Blundelstown 1 (E3075), Co. Meath', *in* E Danaher, *Report on the Archaeological Excavation of Blundelstown 1, Co. Meath* (http://www.m3motorway.ie/Archaeology/Section2/Blundelstown1/file,16730,en.pdf, accessed November 2009).

Sternke, F 2009c *Lithics Finds Report for E3632 Whitehall/Paulstown 2 (A032/146), Co. Kilkenny/Tipperary North Riding—N9/N10 Road Scheme, Knocktopher to Powerstown, Phase 4B*. Unpublished finds report for Irish Archaeological Consultancy Ltd on behalf of Kilkenny County Council.

Sternke, F (in prep. a) 'The stone tool assemblage', *in* R Cleary (ed.), *Neolithic Settlement in North Munster: archaeological excavation at Tullahedy, Co. Tipperary*.

Sternke, F (in prep. b) 'Stuck between a rock and a hard place: skill transmission and differential raw material use in Mesolithic Ireland', *Lithic Technology* (Special Volume).

Sternke, F & Sørensen, M 2009 'The identification of children's flintknapping products in Mesolithic Scandinavia', *in* S McCartan, R Schulting, G Warren & P Woodman (eds), *Mesolithic Horizons: papers presented at the Seventh International Conference on the Mesolithic in Europe, Belfast 2005*, 722–9. Oxbow, Oxford.

Stevens, P 2005 'Killoran 10', *in* M Gowen, J Ó Néill & M Phillips (eds), *The Lisheen Mine Archaeological Project 1996–8*, 292–4. Wordwell, Bray.

Stevens, P 2006 'A monastic enclosure site at Clonfad, Co Westmeath', *Archaeology Ireland*, Vol. 20, No. 2, 8–11.

Stevens, P 2007a *Archaeological Excavations (A003/020, E3502), Ask Sites 42, 43 and 44. N11 Gorey to Arklow Link, Co. Wexford*. Unpublished report for Valerie J Keeley Ltd.

Stevens, P 2007b 'Burial and ritual in late prehistory in north Wexford: excavation of a ring-ditch cemetery in Ask townland', *in* J O'Sullivan & M Stanley (eds), *New Routes to the Past*, 35–46. Archaeology and the National Roads Authority Monograph Series No. 4. National Roads Authority, Dublin.

Stevens, P 2007c 'Clonfad 3: a unique glimpse into early monastic life in County Westmeath', *Seanda*, No. 2, 42–3.

Stevens, P (forthcoming) 'Clonfad 3—an industrious monastery', *in* P Stevens & J Channing, *The Early Medieval Archaeology of Central Westmeath: excavations at Rochfort Demesne, Ballykilmore and Clonfad, on the N6/N52 Realignment Scheme*. NRA Scheme Monographs. National Roads Authority, Dublin.

Stout, D 2002 'Skill and cognition in stone tool production: an ethnographic case study from Irian Jaya', *Current Anthropology*, Vol. 43, 693–722.

Stuiver, M & Reimer, P J 1993 'Extended ^{14}C data base and revised CALIB 3.0 ^{14}C age calibration program', *Radiocarbon*, Vol. 35, No. 1, 215–30.

Stuiver, M, Reimer, P J, Bard, E et al. 1998 'IntCal98 Radiocarbon Age Calibration, 24,000–0 cal BP', *Radiocarbon*, Vol. 40, No. 3, 1041–83.

Stuiver, M, Reimer, P J & Reimer, R W 2005 *CALIB 5.0* (http://www.calib.qub.ac.uk/calib/).

Sweetman, P D 1976 'An earthen enclosure at Monknewtown, Slane, Co. Meath', *Proceedings of the Royal Irish Academy*, Vol. 76C, 25–73.

Talma, A S & Vogel, J C 1993 'A simplified approach to calibrating ^{14}C dates', *Radiocarbon*, Vol. 35, No. 2, 317–32.

Taylor, K 2008 'At home and on the road: two Iron Age sites in County Tipperary', *Seanda*, No. 3, 54–5.

Tierney, J 2009 'Life and death in the later Neolithic and early Bronze Age at Ballynacarriga, Co. Cork', *Archaeology Ireland*, Vol. 23, No. 4, 34–8.

Tierney, J, Ryan, M & Richardson, Á 2008 'Beaker settlement: Area 2, Graigueshoneen Td, Licence No. 98E0575', *in* P Johnston, J Kiely & J Tierney, *Near the Bend in the River: the archaeology of the N25 Kilmacthomas realignment*, 33–8. NRA Scheme Monographs 3. National Roads Authority, Dublin.

Tobin, S, Swift, D & Wiggins, K 2004 *Greystones Southern Access Route (GSAR), Co. Wicklow. Sites 6/6a–g, Priestsnewtown. Excavation report. Licence no. 04E0401*. Unpublished report by Judith Carroll and Co. Ltd for Wicklow County Council.

Tylecote, R F 1977 'The Downpatrick bloom', *Journal of the Historical Metallurgy Society*, Vol. 11, No. 2, 83.

Tylecote, R F 1986 *The Prehistory of Metallurgy in the British Isles*. The Institute of Metals, London.

van der Waals, J D 1964 'Neolithic disc wheels in the Netherlands, with a note on the Early Iron Age disc wheels from Ezinge', *Palaeohistoria*, Vol. 10, 103–46.

Waddell, J 1990 *The Bronze Age Burials of Ireland*. Galway University Press, Galway.

Waddell, J 1995 'The Cordoned Urn tradition', *in* I Kinnes & G Varndell (eds), *'Unbaked Urns of Rudely Shape': essays on British and Irish pottery for Ian Longworth*, 113–22. Oxbow Monograph 55. Oxbow, Oxford.

Waddell, J 1998 *The Prehistoric Archaeology of Ireland*. Galway University Press, Galway.

Wallace, A 2008 *Lowpark, Co Mayo*. Unpublished metallurgical report for Mayo County Council.

Wallace, P 1985 'The archaeology of Viking Dublin', *in* H B Clarke & A Simms (eds), *The Comparative History of Urban Origins in Non-Roman Europe*, 103–45. British Archaeological Reports, International Series 255. Oxford.

Walsh, F 2006 'Neolithic Monanny, County Monaghan', *in* J O'Sullivan & M Stanley (eds), *Settlement, Industry and Ritual*, 7–17. Archaeology and the National Roads Authority Monograph Series No. 3. National Roads Authority, Dublin.

Walsh, F 2007 'Tracing the Bronze Age in Tober', *Seanda*, No. 2, 14–15.

Walsh, F 2008 'Killickaweeny 1: high-class early medieval living', *in* N Carlin, L Clarke & F Walsh, *The Archaeology of Life and Death in the Boyne Floodplain: the linear landscape of the M4*, 27–53. NRA Scheme Monographs 2. National Roads Authority, Dublin.

Walsh, F 2009 *N6 Kinnegad–Athlone Road Scheme: Phase 2, Kilbeggan–Athlone Dual Carriageway. Site A016/051; E2677: Tober 1, Co. Offaly*. Unpublished report on behalf of Westmeath County Council.

Walton Rogers, P 1997 *Textile Production at 16–22 Coppergate*. The Archaeology of York: The Small Finds 17/11. Council for British Archaeology, London.

Warner, R 1990 'A proposed adjustment to the "Old Wood Effect"', *in* W G Mook & H T Waterbolk (eds), *Proceedings of the Second Symposium of 14C and Archaeology, Groningen, 1987*, 159–72. Council of Europe, Strasbourg.

Waterman, D M 1954 'Excavations at Clough Castle, Co. Down', *Ulster Journal of Archaeology*, Vol. 17, 103–63.

Waterman, D M 1958 'Excavations at Ballyfounder Rath, Co. Down', *Ulster Journal of Archaeology*, Vol. 21, 39–61.

Waterman, D 1965 'The court cairn at Annaghmare, Co. Armagh', *Ulster Journal of Archaeology*, Vol. 28, 3–46.

White-Marshall, J & Walsh, C 2005 *Illaunloughan Island: an early medieval monastery in County Kerry*. Wordwell, Bray.

Whittaker, J C 2001 '"The Oldest British Industry": continuity and obsolescence in a flintknapper's sample set', *Antiquity*, Vol. 75, No. 228, 382–90.

Whittle, A 1997 *Sacred Mound, Holy Rings: Silbury Hill and the West Kennet palisade enclosures: a later Neolithic complex in north Wiltshire*. Oxbow Monographs in Archaeology. Oxbow, Oxford.

Woodman, P C & Scannell, M 1993 'A context for the Lough Gur lithics', *in* E Shee-Twohig & M Ronayne (eds), *Past Perceptions: the prehistoric archaeology of south-west Ireland*, 53–62. Cork University Press, Cork.

Young, T (forthcoming) 'Exploiting the bog: iron production and metalworking', *in* P Stevens & J Channing, *The Early Medieval Archaeology of Central Westmeath: excavations at Rochfort Demesne, Ballykilmore and Clonfad, on the N6/N52 Realignment Scheme*. NRA Scheme Monographs. National Roads Authority, Dublin.